the thrifty gardener

the thrifty gardener

Alys Fowler

photography by Simon Wheeler

kyle cathie ltd

Contents

The slow track

My best claim to authority is that I love gardening, that I am passionate about plants and that I love dirt and the world around me. But there was a time when this passion drove me elsewhere. One day I found myself sitting at a computer and I lost the plot. Literally lost it, the place where I should have been – out in the dirt growing instead of writing about how others should do it. I'd become someone that would sooner talk about plants than grow them and it needed to be the other way round.

It's an uneasy feeling knowing you're not where you should be. I had a dream job making TV about gardening; this was supposed to be where it was at, but it wasn't. To cut this story short, I changed jobs and went back outside. I met some guys I truly love working with, found a place where I could grow and cook and slowed right down. I joined up as a fully fledged member of the slow movement. I ate slow, travelled slow, gardened slow and even slowed down my bank account. Once I stopped separating my work from my identity, it all fell into place.

This much I've learnt. Gardening is something you do, not something you buy. You don't have to spend money to have a great garden. Slow gardening, like slow food, is taking time to savour. It's the process, not the sudden transformation, that matters. When you build a little, dig a bit, plant a little, harvest often and, more importantly, don't try to do it all at once, nature works with you.

If you find the right plant for the right place, your hardest job is done. Don't try and make a Mediterranean garden if you are somewhere sodden; don't aim for the tropical, if you are somewhere cold. Life has enough pressures without bringing them into the garden. Learn to garden for wildlife as much for yourself, make compost and leaf piles and let nature look after your waste. If you do all this, relax a little, then do a bit more, you'll find you've slowed down enough to really enjoy your garden, wherever it is.

Above and bottom right: My (and many others') spiritual gardening home – 6BC, New York Botanical Garden. Right: The Lower East Side in Manhattan is home to many community gardens, each offering a slither of green calm. Bottom left: The Lower East Side teems with gardening life even if it has happened on the street.

Scrap craft

When I was nineteen, I moved to New York to work at the New York Botanical Garden. I'd never lived in a city before. I was at once entranced and terrified. After what, at the time, I considered a dull country upbringing, the city pulsed with excitement. Yet I couldn't quite accept that I wouldn't have a green place of my own there.

I really searched that city for somewhere to live. When I had almost given up, I wandered into a neighbourhood where every second block seemed to be a garden. I didn't really know where I was, except that I had to stay. I rented a room from a friendly hippie with a top-floor view over all these lovely gardens. One of those gardens was to become my home for that year. I had found a community that was making beautiful gardens literally from the street. This period was perhaps more influential than much of my formal training as a horticulturalist. I fell in love with the ethic, thrift and spirit that thrive in such settings. But mostly I learnt how to scrap craft with great effect.

Scrap craft is when you reuse or recycle unwanted items into something useful. It starts with 'I wonder if I…' and the end result is all sorts of cool stuff for the garden. Floorboards turn into compost bins, a chest of drawers becomes your new container garden and someone's unwanted furniture your new patio table.

It's a way to personalise your own environment without it costing the earth. It's an independent cultural ethos far removed from our commercially driven world.

By being practical and having a set of skills, you can make your world around you, rather than buying someone else's bland version. It's very addictive, partly because there is nothing more satisfying that being able to say 'I did that'. You start to make stuff that suits your home and the way you actually live. And instead of the impersonal elegance or, worse still, the mass ugliness of manufactured things, you get something that says and has a little bit of the spirit and personality of its maker – something made with your own hands for your own pleasure.

Our modern world has become very unrewarding – that long commute to nowhere with the only reward a shopping trip at the weekend. When you grow your own vegetables, make your own teas or recycle your kitchen waste in a bin that you made, you are taking control. You are rewarding yourself instead of waiting for someone else to. You are transforming your world by your rules and, by expressing your life creatively, the unexpected thrives. The best stuff so often comes from the most limited resources. It will take time to find all the boards, beams and screws when you're going after salvage, but it beats going to a store and buying something with no character.

Whatever you end up creating and growing in your garden, find your own way of doing it, and enjoy the process. If you learn anything from this book, it should be that you can grow something; it can be anything, but your world will be even more enriched if it is something that you can sup or sip.

From the ground up

Where are you going to garden?

Before you can grow anything, you need to work out where you're going to do it. If you're lucky you will have a dedicated garden space, but if your garden is not instantly identifiable because it doesn't start from your back door, then you might need a bit of lateral thinking.

There are all sorts of places to garden. If you're on the top floor of a north-facing apartment with no window ledges, then you'll need to borrow your space from elsewhere. If you've got great big windows and plenty of natural light, then you could garden indoors, or maybe you'll have to find some other shared plot. Many older houses and apartments have huge stairwells with a large window begging for at least some spider plants. Or there may be a sliver of land behind the building you're living in; it may be concreted over and housing nothing but rubbish bins, but with a little effort you could turn it into a garden. Community gardens, fire escapes, porches, tiny front gardens, windowsills: all can be put to good use. There are few limitations for those prepared to dream and experiment.

Whatever your space, if you're new to gardening a good way to start is with a few containers. The conditions are controlled and, as long as you remember to give the the plants light and water, you're bound to succeed. Even if you just have a couple of houseplants, a pot on a windowsill with a few herbs in it, or a single tub by your back door, it's a start, and once you have got the hang of a small project you can start tackling bigger ones. You'll find that gardening is a bug that bites quickly. You may have just one pot one day, but before you know it you'll have plants all over the place.

A few key things need to be looked at before you get growing, whether you're starting indoors or out. Firstly, assess how much light you've got, which also determines how hot it's going to get. You cannot grow shade-loving plants in full sun, nor can you do it the other way round. Knowing your light conditions is half the battle. If you're gardening outdoors, even in containers, you also need to think about shelter. Balconies, for example, are very windy, so you will need strong, tough plants that can cope with drying out and won't snap – a good tip is to look for plants that naturally grow in the same exposed conditions, seaside plants happily adapt to life on a balcony.

All plants need water, so you will need a source of water and something to water with – a hose, a bottle, jug or watering can. And all plants need to get their roots into material to grow in, so if you're not gardening in the ground you will need some kind of compost for your containers.

Left: A tiny veg patch in a front garden – pretty and tasty too.

Opposite page: Wind-swept balconies need tough plants such as grasses (top). California poppies (*Eschscholzia californica*) take advantage of even the smallest pockets of soil (bottom).

Design with love

The single key to a stylish garden is love – it's that simple. My work has taken me from grand designs and tiny courtyards, to balconies and sprawling back yards. I think I can safely say I've seen a lot of gardens. The ones that made my heart sing, the ones I can still recall in great detail, all had one thing in common – the people who made, tended and lived in them truly loved them.

Of course, some elements are more stylish than others, and to my mind, some plants beat others by miles for elegance and some are definitely cool. Naff furniture, piles of old plastic pots, old concrete paths and suchlike definitely don't contribute to a stylish space. But on the whole, it's doing your own thing – passionately – that makes a garden work. You need to decide what your style is and work with it. Half the battle with style is adopting the right spirit and following it through with conviction. If plastic gnomes and flaming bedding happen to be your thing, don't let anyone put you off – just go for them unabashedly.

Being fashionable is risky. Fashion is about selling magazines, so what's 'in' one year is going to be 'out' the next. If you think back to those popular nineties' gardens that were all decking and blue glazed balls, you get the point. The only cast-iron rule is to choose the right plant for the right place; there's no point trying to grow sunny plants in shady places, or putting plants that love dry conditions into heavy, wet soil. Otherwise, do your own thing, be a little daring, and be inspired. Confidence and originality will win out in the long run.

Above: **Take time to get to know your space – observation is your most powerful design tool.** Opposite page: **Do a little at a time. Start designing from the back door and work outwards.**

Principles and practice

Having said that, some design formulae are definitely worth looking at. You don't have to abide by them, but the old mantra 'learn the rules before you can break them' stands true. All good gardens follow six golden principles – repetition, variety, balance, emphasis, sequence and scale – in one way or another. On top of these are secondary elements of colour, texture, form or shape and smell. These ideals apply as much to a collection of containers as to any scale of garden.

The truth is that most of us inherit a garden that may have got some basics right and an awful lot wrong. A strong design philosophy is all very well when you have a blank canvas to work from, but it's not so easy when your garden already exists to someone else's design. The best principle of all is always to work slowly.

Never take on the whole garden at once. Start from the back door and work outwards. Take the lawn for instance: you may well have far more than you want, or it may be in the sunniest place which you might prefer to use for vegetables or flowers. But don't rip it all up at once as that would mean a lot of work and digging and weeding. Take it up as you need the space.

Follow the same approach when you're buying plants – take it easy. If you run to the garden centre and max out your credit card on big plants, you may

well come home to find they don't like your windy site or aren't suitable for the afternoon sun. Good design takes time, and that time should be spent learning about your space, your soil and the different aspects of your garden. Discover how the light changes your garden in different seasons, find out how hot it really gets in summer and how much shade falls as the day progresses. Don't rush observation, which is your best design tool of all.

Playing with your space

How you divide your space really matters. All good gardeners know not to show the whole space at once; it's really important to keep an element of surprise. The easiest way to do this is to have a winding path that will reveal new elements around each meander. In a postage-stamp space, you could get the same effect by cleverly placing mirrors to make it look bigger, or by using vertical spaces for hanging or climbing plants.

You can also use verticals to break up space so you can't see the entire garden from one point. Don't be afraid to use tall plants at the front of smaller ones; it adds intrigue. Verbascum, fennel and verbena are examples of tall, see-through plants that add height to plant combinations.

Always plant in odd numbers. Odd numbers of plants always look better than even; it just looks more natural. Check out Mother Nature's own planting style and you'll find a great mass in the middle and a few trailers either side (weeds growing in wasteland all fall into this pattern). This is called a drift. If all you were ever to do was to plant drifts of pleasing colours in your garden, it would look fantastic.

Stick to a very simple palette of hard landscaping materials, but don't rein yourself in when it comes to colour. An all-white garden may be classic, but a little rule-breaking can be a lot of fun. Friction can work wonders and clashing colours can be very cool. Although bedding schemes can smack of the worst of dull municipal planting, if you plant bedding in great masses and allow it to run riot it can look fantastic.

Always remember that your plants' needs come first, not yours. However lovely you think a combination might be, if the plants don't grow in the same conditions it's just not going to happen. You can't plant shade lovers next to sun seekers, and there's no point matching your spring bulbs to your roses because they are never going to appear together. If you want combinations to work, they need to flower at the same time.

Top: **Understand your plant's needs. These California poppies crave sun.** Above: **A winding path reveals the garden slowly.** Opposite: **Use texture, colour and height to give a space body, such as these grasses, see-through *Verbena bonariensis* (right), and pennisetum (left), which begs to be touched.**

The golden principles of design

Repetition: By using a repetition of colour and form, you create movement and flow through the space.

Variety: Choosing a variety of textures and shades of colour will create an element of fascination and intrigue, so that the eye will want to keep looking around.

Balance: A balance of different elements will create harmony within the space. For example, if you use bold, clashing colours, set them against a calming background of green to harmonise the scheme.

Emphasis: The key to emphasis is to keep to a fairly strict use of elements and play them off against each other. This simply means using one element to emphasise another, for example, calm colours such as matt green leaves will highlight interesting stems or bark. Although clashing colours clearly emphasise one another, more subtle hues of the same colour will emphasise brighter ones in a less garish way.

Sequence: How do you physically move through the space? Where does this path lead? What's around that corner? It is about using certain elements to move you towards a focal point.

Scale: You need to consider the context of your space and match the scale of object to that. Putting a tiny alpine next to a huge bamboo will make everything look out of scale.

How to choose a plant

Finding the right plant for the right conditions sounds easy but in practice can be much harder. I confess that I have a great mass of plants by the back door that I couldn't resist buying or taking on, even though I didn't really have appropriate places to put them.

There is often a yawning gap between where you would like a plant to go for aesthetic reasons, and where it really should be put. If you find yourself having to justify a site too forcefully, take a reality check – you're probably just sending that plant to the compost bin. You're also burning a hole in your pocket.

When you go to the garden centre, there are a few things you must think about before you head for the till. The two most vital considerations are what sort of soil the plant needs, and what sort of light conditions. You can meddle with your soil to make it suit the plants' needs, to a degree. Chapter Three gives you the lowdown. But you can't fiddle with light conditions. You either have sun or you don't.

Light matters

All plants need light to make food. Most labels or books tell you how much light a plant needs. These levels are broken down into four categories – full sun, partial shade, light or dappled shade, and deep shade.

Some plants are flexible and can be placated with approximately the right light conditions, but some plants are adamant. A plant that likes full sun can be placed in partial shade, but it will give you fewer flowers and grow slightly lankier stems. A plant that likes partial shade can just about hack a life in full sun as long as its feet are moist during the growing season, but it won't be entirely content. Anything that prefers to grow in deep shade will curl up and die if forced to live its life in the sun, and a plant that needs sun will wilt and die in deep shade.

Above: Hollyhocks (*Alcea rosea*) love full sun and well-drained soil and grow up to 2.5m, so they're perfect for hiding ugly walls or as features in baked spaces.

Get the light right

Full sun means that plants are open to the sun without any shade for most of the day on sunny days. Plants that do well in these areas include drought-loving Mediterranean or desert plants, prairie or meadow plants and alpines.

Lavenders (*Lavandula*) love baking heat, but hate wet feet in winter, so make sure you've got good drainage.

Jerusalem sage (*Phlomis fruticosa*) has furry, grey leaves to trap air and moisture and beat off the midday sun.

Ice plant (*Sedum spectabile*) has dense, flat plates of tiny, star-shaped pink flowers in late summer and thick, fleshy leaves to hold moisture on even the hottest days.

Partial shade refers to areas that are shaded by buildings or trees and shrubs for up to six hours on sunny days. Partial shade is the easiest to work with and many plants thrive in these conditions.

Most gardens are in partial shade and only really committed sun- or shade-lovers fail in these conditions. Shade that lasts only for three hours or less is particularly good for flowering and fruiting plants.

There are huge amounts of plants in this group, some easy examples include lady's mantle (*Alchemilla mollis*) with lovely foliage and acid green flowers, aquilegias or granny's bonnet, and foxgloves (*Digitalis*).

Light shade is often used to describe shade cast by trees, shade that is dappled and creates a moving patchwork of light and shadows.

Dappled shade usually exists only from late spring to early autumn; once the leaves have dropped from the trees the area will be in low winter light. Light shade is most suited to woodland plants in the summer and spring bulbs that finish flowering before the trees are in leaf.

Wood anemone (*Anemone nemerosa*) is a low-growing perennial that creeps along the woodland floor. With lovely, showy, white flowers, it makes the most of what spring sun it finds.

Bleeding heart (*Dicentra spectabilis*) is a showy, clump-forming perennial that flowers in early summer. Striking, nodding, heart-shaped flowers have rose-pink outer petals and white inner ones.

Deep shade is usually caused by tall buildings or dense, evergreen vegetation. Little or no light reaches these areas during the growing season. A good example is at the base of an evergreen hedge, such as leylandii (x *Cupressocyparis leylandii*) or below a north-facing, tall building. Few plants grow happily here, except some ferns and woodland plants.

Lamium galeobdolon 'Silver Spangles' takes brutal dry shade in its stride.

Hedera helix 'Glacier' is a variegated cream and silver ivy that toughs it out against shady walls.

Euonymus fortunei 'Emerald 'n' Gold' or 'Silver Queen' are both candidates to send plant snobs into hysterics. They may be garish, but they are also wildly adaptable and take on any conditions except waterlogging. They can even be sculpted into hedges.

Lesser periwinkle (*Vinca minor*) is an invasive beast in most gardens, but if your city back garden is nothing but thin soil and shade you may be grateful for it.

Surviving the garden centre

Like any shopping experience, it's easy to get whipped into a frenzy of buying at the garden centre and come out with lots of things you neither want or need. Personally, if you are going to spend money anywhere in your garden, I think it should be on plants, as long as you choose wisely. Even a special plant usually costs less than a pizza for two or a night on the town and they'll be gone in a matter of hours. A well-loved plant can be with you for years, a lifetime or even beyond. However, thrift is at the heart of this book, and you should never spend money where it's not needed.

Check the label

When you're choosing plants, the first thing to check is what's on the label. A good plant label tells you an awful lot. Unfortunately, there are a lot of bad labels out there. Every label should have a Latin plant name and, where appropriate, a common one.

We have Carl Linnaeus to thank for universal Latin names. He was an 18th-century Swedish scientist who loved order, so he came up with the binomial naming system which we've used ever since. He gave every plant a family name (genus) and a first name (species). Take the snowdrop (this is its common name). Under the Linnaean system, it is called *Galanthus* (genus) *nivalis* (species). Often the species name hints at what the plant looks like or where it grows, so *nivalis* translates as 'snow-like'.

Naming starts to get a little more complicated, as both nature and humans meddle with things. You start with a species, then nature decides to dabble and you get some variants that have occurred naturally. These may be considered distinct enough to warrant a name, and are often prefixed by the letters 'subsp.' meaning subspecies, 'var.' meaning variety and 'f.' meaning form. The difference between these is semantics at this level,

What's on the label?

Every label should have a Latin name and a common name, and ideally will tell you something about growing conditions, sun, shade, etc and a little about the colour, size and shape.

HHA means half-hardy annual. This means the plant needs heat or it will sulk. It will be around only for one season. Cosmos and many salvias are good examples. They originate from Mexico and germinate in hot, moist conditions, flower in late summer and autumn, and are killed off by the first significant frost.

HA is a hardy annual. These are tough as old boots, but short-term guests who are also only here for a season. For instance, love-in-the-mist (*Nigella damascena*) is sown in autumn, grows slowly over winter and flowers by late spring.

Bedding describes a plant that is used en masse for a showy, but temporary display. Think pansies and tulips, petunias and pelargoniums.

B means biennial. This sticks around for two years, and may seed itself to spring up elsewhere for another two years. The foxglove, (*Digitalis purpurea*) spends year one as a rosette of leaves and year two as a towering purple spire, then seeds itself all over the place.

P is perennial. Perennial plants are here to stay unless the label says 'short-lived perennial', in which case it may last only three years or so. Examples of long-lived perennials include hardy geraniums, day lilies (*Hemerocallis*), peonies (*Paeonia*) and balloon flower (*Platycodon grandiflorus*). Short-lived perennials include columbine or granny's bonnet (*Aquilegia*), delphiniums, Iceland poppies (*Papaver nudicaule*) and pinks (*Dianthus*).

you just need to know they have occurred naturally. When humans decide to dabble, we create cultivars. These are selected, and artificially raised, distinct variants of the species, and we like to give them vernacular names such as *Galanthus nivalis* 'Pusey Green Tips'.

Horticultural lingo

Labels rarely have very detailed information. To make sure you're choosing something that will suit your space, ask a nursery person; they should be able to tell you more about a plant's needs and how it grows.

Euphemisms

- Prolific self-seeder is a plant that will make its way into all sorts of unwanted places. If it weren't pretty, it would be called a weed.
- Rampant means that it will quickly colonise an area, usually by spreading roots, and you may spend the rest of your time pulling it out.
- Tender usually means it can't cope with temperature less than 5°C.

Health check

Make sure your plant is in good condition and worth paying the full price for. Leaves should have a good green colour, no brown tips, no curling edges, no brown or black spots and no necrotic bits (that means dead bits in the middle or edges of leaves).

There should be no bare stems on a plant, unless it's winter, and no damaged tips or broken stems. The soil should be clean, with no green mat growing on the top – that means it's been sitting around too long.

Make sure there are no obvious signs of pest damage – so no munched bits (particularly at the edges as this is a sign of vine weevil, a hideous thing that loves the garden centre), no eggs, no critters running around, no webbing and no sticky residue on the surface of the leaves since this means aphids.

If a plant is small enough to handle, take it out of the pot and check the roots – any garden centre that stops you from doing this isn't worth visiting. There should be healthy, white roots and plenty of soil visible. If roots are spiralling around a hard, central core of soil, this means the plant is rootbound and has sat in the pot for too long. Rootbound plants have a hard time getting established in the garden and often die.

Don't be too seduced by flowers. Although we do it all the time, plants don't actually respond brilliantly to being planted in flower. Plus you'll get more out of a plant that's not flowering its socks off because you'll get a longer display.

Size and space

Some growers plant lots of young plants together in a 5-litre pot to make them look like a single, more mature plant. If you are careful and gently tease them apart, you can often get three or more smaller plants. They'll need some love and good compost, but they'll thank you for their new space and grow away quickly. This is sometimes done with perennials, and always with house palms, when growers germinate up to ten or so seeds per pot. The young seedlings grow up together to produce an impressive thicket, but after several years they all look very unhappy, as they have no room to grow. Instead of waiting for this to happen, repot the seedlings into large (10-litre) pots, with no more than five seedlings per pot, carefully spaced apart.

Opposite page: **Three *Primula denticulata* have been squeezed into one pot to make a bigger-looking plant. Carefully tease the individual plants apart. Next plant each into their new home with good-quality compost. Sit back and admire your thrifty work.**

Bargain hunting

Many garden centres have a reduced-price plant area. You'll have to hunt to find it, usually tucked away at the back. Here the plants are probably covered in liverworts (the green mat on top of the potting compost), and they may be struggling a little with life. But with love, some new compost, a trim to shear off dead stuff, and a little feeding, you'll be surprised what will grow. Try always to knock the plant out of the pot before you take it home to make sure that there are no white grubs or small, evil-looking weevils with shiny shells hiding inside. Those are probably vine weevils and you don't ever want to let them near your garden.

Shop around. I know it sounds obvious, but for some reason people don't seem to do this with plants. So many growers offer mail-order plants online, so do a price comparison. It's not only garden centres that offer seeds these days – you can find plants elsewhere too. Check out pound stores, supermarkets and ironmongers. Look out at car boots and yard sales. If you want home-grown plants, the internet is a good place to look for independent growers and small specialist nurseries. Plant fairs are good for unusual stuff; your local one may advertise online. Some supermarkets sell amazingly cheap houseplants and sometimes genuinely interesting low-cost bulbs.

Opposite page: A good garden centre will offer clever design combos, but make sure you know the final size of each plant. The eucalyptus at the back becomes a huge tree if not pruned. Left: Check the quality of each plant for good colour and growth. Below left: Young plants often establish better than mature ones in flower.

The renter's garden

Renters tend to get the worst deal from gardening and, unless you're going to stay for a while, putting lots of effort into a weedy, overgrown patch can seem a little pointless. Think of it this way: it's not just good exercise but also, if you leave the garden a nice place, then the next renters may have a go too – consider it renters' pride. I spent months rescuing one garden only to find the next lot of renters completely uninterested. I felt completely disheartened, but I cycled by recently and found new renters had moved in and filled all the pots I'd left behind with new flowers in the front. I hope they found the veg garden. I'm still very proud that I cleared that garden of weeds.

Another option is to have a container garden that you take with you. But if you have some ground and want to have a go, some plants are cheap and showy enough to gloss over the problems of a renter's garden.

Budget bulbs

In autumn, all kinds of shops, from DIY stores to supermarkets, offer great bags of mixed daffodil bulbs. These bags contain daffodils in all sizes and shapes, although most will be the large, bright yellow, trumpeted kinds – but they are truly lovely when you cut them and take them inside. As they're so cheap, you can indulge yourself and treat them as cut flowers.

Provided that your soil passes as anything near garden quality (more in Chapter Three), daffodil bulbs will grow, even through the lawn, so you can plant them in great drifts and mow them away by the time you want to sunbathe. The easiest way to determine how deep to plant a bulb is to dig down roughly three times the depth of the bulb. If you plant daffodils too close to the surface, they often fail to flower.

If you've got the space, in order to make a display look as natural as possible, put your bulbs in a bucket and then throw the contents as if you were getting rid of water. A mass will land together, a smaller number will make it farther, like trailing stars. Wherever the bulbs land, plant them. In lawns, cut out three sides of a square and hinge back the turf, chuck in a few bulbs and firm the turf back again. In beds and borders in soft autumn soil, just put your fork in and wriggle to make a hole big enough to put the bulb in.

Price is a good indication of how easy the bulb is to grow: the cheaper the price, the easier it tends to be. The best bulbs go first, so as soon as you see garden centres and supermarkets stocking them, start buying – the bigger the bulb, the better the flowers. A good healthy bulb feels plump, firm and not withered, has no signs of damage and no mould growing on it. If it's squidgy, it's probably going to rot in the ground. Don't wait around to plant them. However, if you've got lots to plant, leave your tulips till last, just make sure they're in before the end of December.

Bulbs to look out for

Flowering January to March

Plant spring- and early summer-flowering bulbs in autumn. *Snowdrops* (*Galanthus*) are technically better grown 'in the green' (meaning you plant them with leaves on), but I've never seen these in a city. Buy dry, buy cheap and be patient as they may take a little time to get going.

Crocuses are as cheap as chips and can be grown in grass, so make the lawn a little more interesting. Once established, they slowly colonise a lawn.

Muscari or grape hyacinth are very early flowering bulbs, with flowers that look like small bunches of deep blue grapes. They like an open, well-drained site.

Flowering April to June

The trick with cheap *tulips* is to treat them like bedding as they tend not to flower well the following year. Plant them near the surface, 5–8cm (2–3in) deep, then they are easy to pull out once they've finished flowering.

Hyacinths are so easy you can grow them in pure water. Cheap mixed packs of hyacinths are for the brave as you'll get lots of very garish pinks and purples as well as blues. More restrained gardeners should only go for white or blue cultivars.

Flowering July to September

Cyclamen hederifolium is good for dry areas of the garden and best planted under trees or shrubs. Often sold as dry, flat discs, the bulbs can take time to establish, so if you're not staying more than a year or two, consider them as presents for the next lot. Once the bulbs get established, they'll self-seed all over the place. Plant them as soon as you see them for sale, usually in late summer.

naked ladies or autumn crocuses (*Colchicum speciosum*) have very striking, large crocus-like flowers. They need full sun and well-drained soil. Plant these in summer or early autumn.

Flowering October to December

Crocus speciosus grow very happily in areas that are dry in summer, preferring full sun and happy in gritty soil. Good for poor, urban soils, these flower in late autumn as the soon as soil temperature drops and moisture increases. Plant them in late summer.

Opposite page: **How to create a natural-looking drift of bulbs. Put the bulbs in a bowl and then toss them out. Wherever they land, plant them.** Right: **Daffodils can look a little municipal, but they are lovely in vases and will make shabby grass look vibrant in spring.**

Unfussy candidates

With all plants, it's a good idea to clear weeds as much as you can before planting or sowing. But if you really don't have the time and energy to convert a neglected patch into a perfect growing space, some plants are tough. With a little love at the early stages, some food and a little water, they will quickly start to out-compete weeds and transform your rented patch. Annuals grow fast and establish quickly, so if you're only around for a season or two, choose nasturtiums and poppies.

Mallows are tough, long flowering and unfussy. They range from vigorous, easy shrubs, such as the pretty tree mallow *Lavatera* x *clementii* 'Barnsley', to appealing annual varieties, such as *Lavatera trimestris* 'Loveliness'. This old variety has seen a comeback in recent years and will hold its own against most weeds. It's a big, upright plant that will grow to 1m tall, with lots of lovely showy, saucer shaped, deep pink flowers. Sow the seeds in mid to late spring, 15cm apart in furrows (ridges of seed-friendly soil) with 30cm in between rows. Mallows make an impressive display even on poor soil and their bulky foliage helps to keep further weeds in check. If all you manage in your first year is a few mallows, you won't be disappointed.

Opium poppy (*Papaver somniferum*) is an impressive, blowsy annual that will grow to a height and size to hide a multitude of sins. A mass of poppies will lift your eye rather than letting it linger on a horrid path or a bunch of weeds. The flowers are most often in various hues of pinkish purple, veering occasionally into red and almost black which are followed by attractive seedheads, extending their interest well into autumn. Someone, somewhere, in your neighbourhood is bound to have plants and therefore quantities of seed, but if you do have to buy seeds it will be a once-only purchase as one plant provides more than enough for the following year.

Opposite page: Shrubby perennial *Lavateras* grow quickly and flower from mid-summer to autumn. Grow in a sunny, sheltered spot with well-drained soil. Particularly good for front gardens in polluted areas as these guys are tough.

Right: Wherever the seed is scattered in sunny spots, the corn poppy (*Papaver rhoeas*) makes its home.

If you manage to secure a good quantity of seed, perhaps if you have saved some from last year, the best way to sow it is to throw a handful a week liberally around your garden from mid-February till early May. This way all your poppies won't flower at once. Opium poppies do need bare ground to germinate, which is partly why you start chucking them down in February when little else is up. You may need to take a hoe or spade and rough up the ground a little before sprinkling them on the surface. Never bury the seed or it won't germinate.

Single and double Shirley poppies

A form of the corn or field poppy, *Papaver rhoeas*, these flower slightly earlier than opium poppies and are slightly shorter. Sow the two types together for a long display. Look out for the salmon-pink strains of Shirley poppies because they blend in well.

Nasturtiums will scramble over the worst weeds and will take the thin, baked soil of many back gardens. They're as cheap as chips from seed and there are many weird and wonderful varieties out there. I think the deep red colours are really quite glamorous.

It's hard not to fall in love with hardy *geraniums*. These should not be confused with their cousins the Pelargoniums, which are less hardy and grow indoors. Hardy geraniums are a little bit of a step up in the garden world, a little more discerning but, boy, do they work hard. They can withstand shade, but most don't mind taking full sun, which makes them great for urban gardens that bake half the day and then spend the other half in the shade of buildings. They don't mind dry conditions and, given a little love, will flower their socks off. Give them a Chelsea chop (see p. 124), cut them right back by the end of June, and they'll flower right the way through to October. It's a large genus and there is at least one variety for every garden, whether small, large, damp or shady.

Geranium macrorrhizum naturally grows among rocks and scrub, usually in the shade, in the mountains of Europe. All this means it's perfect ground cover – meaning less weeding – for dry shade in the garden. It spreads to 45cm tall and 60cm wide with pink to purplish-pink flowers and aromatic foliage that turns red and yellow before it drops in autumn. *Geranium* x *cantabrigiense* is another

excellent value plant, growing to 15cm tall and 30cm wide. It has slightly scented, evergreen foliage, bright pink or purple flowers and creates a dense carpet of light green foliage. It's good for ground cover in sun or shade and flowers from June to July. *Geranium phaeum* 'Album' is another good plant for shade or semi-shade. It grows into tall clumps, 80cm high and 40cm wide. In mild areas of 5°C and above, it tends to keep its leaves during winter and flowers from May to June, with a second flush later if left to its own devices. The leaves usually have rather attractive, purple splodges on them. I prefer the white-flowering 'Album' to the straight *Geranium phaeum*, which can be a bit of a muddy, cheerless shade of purplish red.

No-
garden
gardening

Container choices

Containers laugh in the face of anyone who says they can't garden because they haven't got space. With a few containers, you can make a garden on a balcony, fire escape or roof-top, in a concrete courtyard or in those weird, unclaimed spaces at the backs of offices. If you're renting, containers give you the chance to indulge in gardening, then take the whole thing with you when you move on.

Many of us start our gardening love affair with containers and it's a great place to start because you can control the conditions. Sometimes you may have space outside your home, but may still prefer to garden in containers. They allow you to have a garden even if you have a problem with the local cats, if your site has been contaminated in the past, or if your soil is little more than rubble. I've finally got soil, but I certainly haven't given up my containers.

Once you've decided you want to grow in containers, where do you start? Treat gardening with containers the same way as any other kind of gardening. It's hard to make a jumble of plastic pots look stylish, but there are all sorts of other things you can use to grow plants in. It's best either to be restrained and minimalist or eccentrically eclectic; you could use just one type of container or go for everything and anything that will house a plant, as long as you have flair and a good eye – no old boots or loo basins!

Wine boxes, with their lovely embossed logos, are great for growing salad crops in. The best place to get them is from high-end wine merchants as the better the wine, the better the quality of box. Portuguese port boxes are usually really well made. It's a good idea to add corner braces to stop the wood from warping and you need to preserve the wood with something like Danish oil to weatherproof it. You also need to drill holes in the base for drainage. You can happily grow radishes, cut-and-come-again lettuces, spring onions, Oriental greens, tomatoes and herbs in boxes.

Another good source is old drawers. These tend to be made from very good wood with lovely dovetailed joints. Again, you'll need to weatherproof and create drainage holes; you should also line the drawers with plastic because they were never meant to be used outside, and brace the corners. Big drawers around 20–30cm deep are the best find as you can grow roots such as beetroot, turnips, swedes or an entire salad crop in one box.

Preparing wooden containers

All wooden containers need preserving. Oil waterproofs the wood while still allowing it to breathe, so if the wood gets wet it can dry out. I use Danish oil, which is a blend of various oils that dry to form

Left: **Salad boxes – wooden boxes make stylish homes for summer salads. Whether it's an old drawer or a funky wine box, you can grow a summer-long supply of leaves and greens.**

a hard surface. You'll need at least three coats and it's not worth cutting corners because the more layers you treat it with, the longer the wood will last. A cheaper option is boiled linseed oil, but this takes over a week to dry properly and can have a sticky finish – I've found that it works well on wine boxes, as this wood is so dry that it just sucks it in, but it's no good on pre-treated wood.

Don't be tempted to varnish your boxes, as this will only provide more work. Varnish creates an impervious layer that physically keeps water out, but if there is any sort of crack then water gets in but can't get out, then the wood rots from the inside.

Tins, sacks and bags

Large food tins make brilliant growing containers. Among my favourites are the big square ones containing bulk-cured olives, with lovely designs on the front. You may be able to get hold of them from a market stall that sells olives. Or try asking restaurants for ghee or oil tins. You'll have to cut the top off them and inevitably they'll rust, but that can be a good look. Drill holes near the bottom around the sides, rather than through the base, for the best drainage.

Dried baby formula or large coffee tins make good small containers for herbs. Rip off the labels and paint them. Poke holes in the bottoms with a large nail and arrange a whole group along the top of a wall or windowsill. Biscuit tins work well too. There are some fantastic retro versions out there and all are good for growing shallow-rooting things, such as alpines or succulents.

Potatoes grow so easily in containers that I've almost given up growing them in the ground. I bought five very large pots (the size of dustbins, another alternative) from a pound store a couple of years ago

and grow a summer supply with virtually no effort. Spuds will grow equally as well in old compost or mulch bags. These can be disguised with hessian sacks. Some of the nicest are seed potato bags, so ask your garden centre if they have any when you buy your potatoes in spring. Another source of sacks is pet stores who may get bulk supplies of peanuts in them.

The very cheapest container is not stylish, but it makes up for this in practicality and price – the plastic bag. You can grow almost anything in a plastic bag, as long as it's not see-through because roots don't like light. One trick is to use compost bags as containers. Buy small to medium multi-purpose mix for containers and just open up the top, poke some drainage holes in the bottom and away you go. You can grow tomatoes, courgettes, potatoes, chard and peas this way. I've seen vegetables and flowering plants successfully grown in supermarket plastic bags. It may not be attractive, but if you know that you're only renting a flat for six months or so and don't want the hassle of transporting pots, it's one way to have a garden.

Opposite page:
Harvesting potatoes.
Remove haulms and
tip contents out onto a
groundsheet.
Centre: **From one**
potato comes many.
See The Directory
for how to grow.
Right: **Oil tins are a**
funky alternative to
plastic pots.

Potting compost

Containers require good potting compost that holds moisture but drains well, and has a good structure so it doesn't go dense and soggy when it's wet. This is particularly important because containers undergo heavy watering and air is as important to roots as water. It is perfectly possible to make your own potting compost from scratch, using loam, home-made compost, sand and leaf mould, but if you have a small space it's not that practical as you have to store all the individual ingredients. It's often easier to buy the right stuff for the job.

Most container-grown plants do best in loam-based compost. Loam is a fertile soil that is made up of more or less equal parts clays, sand and silt. Shop-bought loam is always sterilised so it is free of bacteria and potential diseases.

A standard range of potting composts were developed in the 1930s by the John Innes Foundation. The composts are called No.1, No.2 and No.3 and each suits a specific range of plants and situations. The main ingredients are loam, peat or a peat-free alternative and sand.

No.1 is ideal for seedlings; it has an open structure and is ideal for germination as it allows light and moisture to move freely through the compost and doesn't contain much food. Seeds don't actually require nutrients at the initial stages of germination, as the seed itself does all the feeding.

No.2 is suitable for larger, establishing plants. Use it for potting on young seedlings and taking cuttings. No.2 has twice as much fertiliser in the mix because young plants need a rich diet to get going.

No.3 is for long-term established plants, so it's the best choice for containers. It contains enough fertiliser to keep plants going for the long haul.

Stay away from peat

At this stage it is all very simple, but there are still choices to make. You can have peat-based compost or a peat-free alternative. Please, for the planet's sake, don't use peat. It is neither economically or environmentally sustainable. Peat is a truly amazing substrate – it is inert, porous and helps provides ideal growing conditions – so there is a great deal of reluctance to give it up. But there are good alternatives, many of them made from coir (a by-product of the coconut industry) or green waste. Coir absorbs water well and is free-draining like peat; some say it is a bit too free-draining to use for seeds and seedlings, but it is quick to re-absorb water, so is an ideal alternative if you keep a close eye on watering. So-called 'green waste' can be a blend of anything from shredded pallets or chicken feathers to garden waste collected by the council for recycling. The trick is not to treat peat-free alternatives in the same way as peat. Peat-free alternatives have different qualities, so you should check when you buy them whether you need to treat them any differently from peat-based composts.

The John Innes system is easy to understand, but manufacturers wanted something even easier. So they came up with multi-purpose compost, which somehow manages to meet all the requirements – sort of. It's a bit of a 'Jack of all trades, master of none'. You can use it for seed sowing and for cuttings, but it won't necessarily give your plants the best start. It is a good choice for containers, but tends to contain a limited supply of food. If you can buy only one bag of compost, then buy peat-free multi-purpose, but if you have room to buy another type too, then buy a bag of No.1 as it's the most usefully different.

As a rule of thumb, it is always best to amend multi-purpose compost. For seedlings, you need to add structure to the mix. I add roughly 50 per cent sand and vermiculite in equal parts. Vermiculite is a natural volcanic product that holds on to water and releases it as the plants need it. For cuttings, I tend to add around 25–50 per cent horticultural grit, depending on the plants' requirements. I also use special mixes for specific groups of container-grown plants.

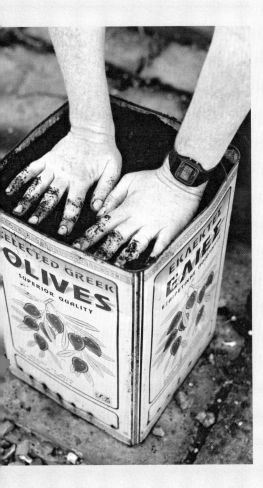

Specific compost mixes

Free-draining mix for succulents, Mediterranean plants and cacti

2 parts multi-purpose compost

1 part grit

1 part horticultural sand

1 handful (per pot) of slow-release food, such as chicken manure pellets

General compost mix for vegetables and flowers

4 parts multi-purpose compost

1 part vermiculite

2 parts composted fine bark

1 handful (per pot) of slow-release food, such as chicken manure pellets

Super-light mix for roof-tops and balconies

You need to water plants on roofs and exposed places more frequently. They will be subject to winds, so tend to dry out faster. Any lightweight compost mix, by its nature, will dry out fast so containers must be watered often.

2 parts multi-purpose compost

1 part vermiculite or perlite (vermiculite holds water better. Perlite is another very porous volcanic product; it can be dusty so watch out if you're asthmatic.)

1 part polystyrene (this has no nutritional value at all, but it's light, adds lots of drainage and it's free. Polystyrene nuggets are used as packaging in lots of parcels. Look in skips as you get loads of it around new white goods.)

2 parts composted fine bark

1 handful (per pot) of slow-release food, such as chicken manure pellets

Right: Beginners choice. Garlic is easy to grow in a container. Plant individual bulbs in autumn and shoots will appear before Christmas. See The Directory for growing info.

Opposite page: Champagne boxes are ideal for window ledges.

Container harvests

Plants in containers rely on you for all their needs, so you do need to look after them. You can grow several crops in one pot in swift succession as long as you keep the plants well fed. Every time you start new seedlings, remember to refresh the pot by adding plenty of food in the form of fresh compost. The best stuff is from your compost bin – add a new layer and mix it into the existing material.

In hot weather, you'll need to water vegetables every day. If you can't, then try growing food that you can crop before the hottest weather such as rocket, potatoes and rhubarb, which is quite happy in a large container. Water early in the morning before you go to work as the plant will use this water most effectively. Half a litre (1 pint) at seven in the morning equates to ten by midday. Watering in the evening is almost as good.

Successional growing

By sowing little and often throughout the season you can have a summer-long supply of fast-growing crops, such as radishes, lettuces and peas. A common mistake is to sow too much at any one time and be left with a glut. As soon as one sowing has raised its head above ground, it's time to start the next to ensure a harvest over several months.

Admittedly, it's hard to do this when all you have is a few pots, but one successful way is to grow your seedlings in modules. These are seed trays divided into squares big enough to grow one seedling in a plug of compost. You'll have to allow a four- to five-week gap between sowings, rather than the two to three weeks you need when you have plenty of container space. As you harvest, say, one lettuce, you add some more compost and plant the next plug in the hole you have made by harvesting. If you can't be bothered or you don't feel you're organised enough to have lots of germinating seed trays and on-going plugs, sow one half of a pot or box, wait a couple of weeks and sow the other half.

Salad specials

Containers make happy homes for plenty of vegetables (see Chapter Nine), but salads are perhaps the most rewarding. They are really simple to grow and, with a little effort, you can keep at least one box growing through a mild winter. If you can stop buying washed bags of salad for even half a year to pick your own fresh stuff, that's a huge achievement.

Lettuce is a dream to sow. Just water the container, scatter the slender seeds across the surface, cover them with just enough compost to

hide them, and away they'll grow. There are fantastic varieties of lettuce out there, much more tasty than those you find in the supermarkets. Lettuces fall into two broad categories: hearting and loose-leaf types. Once you discover the differences, you'll soon be hunting for that classic blond Batavian 'Pierre Bénite' or that rare Czech heirloom 'Lednicky'. Until then, there are plenty of others to keep your tastebuds happy.

Loose-leaf lettuces are the best for small spaces. They can be grown as cut-and-come-again crops (CCA), which is when you simply shear the rows of lettuces at 5–10cm tall, rather than letting them mature. This will give you bowls full of tasty little leaves in around a month from sowing. Three weeks after the first cuts, you'll be able to cut again and, if it's not baking hot you can get a third and even a fourth cut. If you have a second box that you have sown two weeks after the first, you'll have a supply for months.

In very hot conditions, lettuce leaves become coarse or the plants bolt (go to seed), so sow from late spring until early summer and again from late summer into autumn. Space the seeds 1cm apart in a wide drill – which means an indented line in the soil – leaving about 10cm between rows. If you are sowing in a round pot, liberally scatter a small amount of seeds on the surface. Look for lettuce seed packets labelled 'Cut-and-Come-Again', 'Leaf bowl' or 'Salad bowl'.

If you hanker after crisp heads of lettuce sow cos or butterhead types for late spring and early summer, then later in the year any types except butterhead, which wilt in heat. Heads of lettuce are lovely, but once you've cut the head off, that's it. If you only want enough at any one time for a sandwich, then you can make each head last longer by harvesting just the outside leaves. Hearting lettuces need to be thinned to about 15cm apart when the plants are big enough to handle – eat the thinnings – and take about three months to mature into a full grown crispy head.

Lettuce bolts in hot weather, and what was a short, round plant quickly turns into a towering alien. At the end of the season, I like to let some of my plants go in order to collect seed for next year or just to enjoy the look and add a new dimension to the container garden.

Currently saladini, also known as mesclun or misticanza, are hugely popular. These are salad mixes containing all sorts of seeds, including pak choi, tat soi, mizuna, red kale, mustard, rocket, komatsuna, Chinese leaf, corn salad and endive. They look great with plenty of reds and vibrant greens in the mixes. Oriental mixes are more spicy than Mediterranean versions. Sow them just like CCA lettuce and you'll be able to harvest them for many months before they go coarse. In an Oriental mix, the coarse leaves are great for stir-fries. With planning and a crop cover in the form of fleece or bubblewrap, you can sow outdoors as late as October. I like to have a spicy saladini and a CCA lettuce wine box on the go, sown roughly two weeks apart. That way I alternate between spicy and calm.

Other great container greens include rocket, which pleasingly shoots to maturity quicker than anything; winter purslane or miner's lettuce which goes right through a mild winter; lamb's lettuce, mibuna and mizuna, red mustard and endives, which are good to look at and eat.

Winter harvest

Although most plants stop growing below 6° C, there are plenty that can make it even down to −5°C, so if you're somewhere mild, try keeping some boxes of greens going with a bit of bubblewrap for protection. Where it's too cold, or if space is at a premium, go for windowsill cut-and-come-again seedlings.

You'll need to make roughly three sowings: one at the beginning of September, one in early October and the last in mid February. September sowing is suitable for Oriental greens (spicy mixes of mizuna, rosette pak choi, mustard greens and komatsuna are good) and for cold hardy lettuces such as 'Winter Density' and winter purslane. Coriander, celery, red orache, amaranth and broccoli all make really tasty cut-and-come-again crops.

In October, sow very fast-growing crops such as rocket, cress and mustards. Then in February, sow lettuce indoors, and outside you can make early sowings of rosette pak choi, rocket, spinach, Russian red kale, broccoli and winter purslane. This lot will keep you going while you wait for your spring sowings to get going.

Above: In hot conditions, salads often bolt (flower) and go to seed. Don't worry, just harvest the seed for next year.

Left and right: Protect late-summer salads through a mild winter with bubblewrap. I've used plumber's piping to make a tent.

Window boxes

Everyone who lives in town has one – a favourite street where you turn the corner and there it is, an explosion of colour on someone's windowsill. A good window box doesn't just make a house, it can transform an entire street. And the effect of a window box is not only felt outdoors, inside it softens your view and brings nature right to your window. Even on a thirty-storey tower block, butterflies, bees and birds will happily stop by.

You need a window that can open at the bottom or one that you can easily – and conveniently – reach from outside, such as a fixed basement window, and a windowsill. Even if you have a very deep windowsill, it is vital to fix your window boxes securely; once filled with compost and watered, they become incredibly heavy and could be highly dangerous if they were to fall. You can find ready-made window-box fixings in some ironmongers and online, or adapt hanging-basket fixings to secure a box. Otherwise, make a simple barrier to go across the front length of the sill.

Life on the sill

Windowsills can be harsh environments as they get baked by the sun and ravaged by the wind. Perhaps surprisingly, when it rains, windowsills see little of the water. Couple this with the wind, and the fact that window boxes usually provide rather a shallow rooting area, and you'll realise that plants have to survive very dry conditions. Be sure to choose plants that can cope with these conditions, or you'll be constantly battling. If your windowsill is in deep shade, I'm afraid you may be constantly battling anyway as little will do well. Try spring bulbs and ivy; the former make the most of what they can find before disappearing for summer, the latter finds what light it can by climbing towards it.

In the height of summer you will have to water very regularly, even if you are using drought-tolerant plants. You'll also have to feed your box every two weeks with liquid feed to make sure that the compost maintains enough energy to give the plants what they need for a good display. You need to treat most window-box plantings as seasonal; take the plants out when they have done their thing and start afresh, bringing in new soil and plants. A tired window box is a very sorry sight. If you have space, perennial plants can be given a home elsewhere after one season. If not, pop them straight into the compost and they will still be useful.

Left: These tobacco plants (*Nicotiana*) were found in a bargain basement corner, and with a little love, they flowered their socks off all summer.

Opposite page, top: You can't beat a classic look such as red geraniums for window boxes.

Opposite page, bottom: Be greeted with winter cheer as you head off to work in the morning.

45

Left: **Nasturtiums have colourful, edible flowers and are a perfect choice for a hot, sunny ledge.**

Brick work

If you only have a very narrow, very baked window sill and little inclination to water all the time, but you still want to look out on flowers, the lowest maintenance display of all comes from growing shallow-rooting sedums or sempervivums (houseleeks). These are mountainous plants adapted to grow in very shallow, very poor soil, under extreme conditions from searing heat to bitter cold. They're usually to be found in the alpine section of a garden centre. Sedums, such as *Sedum acre*, *Sedum rupestre* and *Sedum spathulifolium* are mat-forming perennials that are adapted to extreme conditions. They form very dense mats of succulent leaves and then flower their socks off in late summer and early autumn.

The easiest way is to grow them in engineering bricks – the kind with holes in them. Gather together enough bricks to fill your sill and pack half of each hole with a mix of 2 parts good multi-purpose compost with 1 part grit or vermiculite. This is a bit fiddly as the compost will want to fall out, so pack it in as tight as you can. Break a rooted rosette large enough to fill the rest of each hole from each plant, and gently push each one into the compost. Sit each brick in a tray of water until the compost is fully saturated, then put them on your windowsill. If there is any danger of them tumbling off, you should secure wire through the holes before you start and use this to tie the bricks on to a hook attached to the side of the window frame. Eventually the rosettes will smother the bricks and the plants will thrive in this inhospitable environment because the bricks are porous and will absorb and release just the right amount of water. In the hottest weather you can slosh some water over them to help out. You'll have to do a little maintenance every now and then; pick off some dead rosettes and flower stalks, maybe give them a foliage feed once in a while but that's it, and I bet the bees will visit your window sill.

This page: Sempervivums growing in a brick. Carefully tease individual rosettes apart and squeeze into the holes in the brick. Water well and they'll soon anchor themselves in.

Making a window box

Wine boxes, wooden CD racks and skip wood can all be used to knock together a simple window box. If you use wood, or are lucky enough to find an old terracotta box in a skip, you'll need to line the box with something waterproof to conserve water so that plants can make the most of it. I use old compost bags.

As when you're making any kind of container, if you use recycled wooden boxes you need to brace the corners that so the wood won't warp or split. Also drill holes in the bottom for drainage. Cheap plastic window boxes never have drainage holes, so if you use these be sure to poke some in before you start planting. A knife or large nail heated over a gas flame works best to puncture plastic.

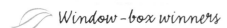

Window-box winners

Plant these on their own or mix them up.

Edible

Sunny sill
Chives, basil (Greek or bush basil work best), parsley, coriander.

Drought-tolerant plants
Thyme, pot marjoram (oregano), sage.

Partly shady sill (north facing for instance)
Parsley, chives (will take some shade), mint (thrives in shady conditions as long as it is well watered, so make sure your compost has some bulky organic matter, such as home-made compost or composted bark, mixed in).

Floral

Sunny sill
Nasturtiums, petunias, geraniums, sedums.

Nicotiana 'Lime Green', French marigolds(*Tagetes patula*), dwarf pinks (*Dianthus chinensis*).

Partly shady sill
Coral flower (*Heuchera sanguinea*) and cultivars, *Primula auricula* (flowers from March to May), winter-flowering heather (*Calluna vulgaris*).

Winter- and early spring-flowering plants
Heather (*Calluna vulgaris*), compact hebes, e.g. 'Youngii', ivy (*Hedera*), violas – underplant with dwarf daffodils (*Narsissus*), crocus or grape hyacinth (*Muscari armeniacum*).

Drought-tolerant plants
Lace aloe (*Aloe aristata*), houseleeks (*Sempervivum*), sedums, crassulas.

Left and opposite page: These lace aloes (*Aloe aristata*) are growing in an old wooden CD rack. These make perfect window boxes for drought-tolerant plants that love free-draining conditions.

49

Indoor gardening

For a long time the only garden I had was an indoor garden, and I can tell you that indoor gardening's really where it's at. It's always seen as the poor relative of 'real' gardening outside, but not a bit of it. It's high time for it to come out and shine.

Planting a healthy home

As you battle your way home through taxis, buses and cars, you may think that all the bad air is outside, but the sad truth is that things aren't that rosy indoors either. Some research suggests that our indoor environment can actually be up to ten times more polluted than outdoors. A hundred years ago, our homes were full of natural materials, lots of wood: wool and cotton textiles, and a few bits of metal. Nowadays, we've surrounded ourselves with a crazy load of chemicals.

You'll have guessed where I'm heading. Don't spend hundreds on air purifiers and extractors, but get some houseplants. It sounds ludicrously simple, but plants are the best air conditioners out there. The most effective air-purifying plants come from the tropics.

Left: My avocado and snake plant (*Sansevieria trifasciata*) keeping each other happy. No-one can kill a snake plant, so every house should have one. Opposite page: How I love this Golden Pothos plant (*Epipremnum aureum*), which has made its way across my friend Silvia's office.

Indoor pollutant busters

Areca palm *Chrysalidocarpus lutescens*

Lady palm *Rhapis excelsa*

Rubber plant *Ficus elastica* **'Robusta'**

Dragon plant *Dracaena* **spp.**

English ivy *Hedera helix*

Peace lily *Spathiphyllum* **spp.**

Gerbera daisy *Gerbera jamesonii*

Spider plant *Chlorophytum comosum*

These plants have evolved to have unusually high transpiration rates (transpiration is the evaporation of water from plants and how plants move water through their system). This allows them to survive under the dimly lit canopy of the forest – an environment that in lots of ways resembles our homes and offices, with fairly low light and warm temperatures.

The needs of your indoor plants

All plants, whatever their function in your home, need three things to be happy, just like plants outside – light, water and food. Light indoors can be tricky as you can never fully replicate the light that is found in the plants' natural habitat, But it's perfectly possible to work with your available light to please your plants.

We tend to think about rooms as being either light or dark, but this is oversimplistic. Even in a light room, there will be a limited source of direct light, perhaps 1.7–2m from the window. The rest of the room will be in shade, but if there are pale walls light will be reflected round the room.

Plants grown in too little light become leggy and, if they are really deprived of light, they die. A leggy plant develops a long stem and small leaves. It will also bend to grow in the direction of the light source – this is called phototropism. Ideally plants want light to come from all directions, including directly from above, but as this is rarely possible indoors a plant reacts by

turning towards the light. To counteract, this you have to turn the pot regularly so that the plant gets a fairly even amount of light on all sides. Then it should grow directly upright.

Although we notice the difference in the amount of light from summer to winter, our eyes are not subtle enough to estimate the scale of the difference. As days get longer (from early spring onwards), don't close your curtains at night – those few extra minutes each morning make a huge difference to your houseplants. Ideally, plants should be kept in front of curtains; it can get a bit cold behind.

At the other extreme, a south-facing window can be bathed in very intense light in summer. Only cacti can really stand such conditions; other houseplants should be moved about 1m from the window so that they don't scorch.

Your houseplants will love you dearly if you can give them a summer residence outside. If the summer temperatures are above 15°C, then houseplants can go out. If you have a balcony or patio, move them out but acclimatise them gently to the bright outside light by starting them in the shade until their tender indoor leaves have got used to the outside world. A spell outdoors gives them a chance to catch real rays, and to get battered a little by wind and rain. They will respond by growing that bit tougher, making them all the stronger for winter.

Opposite page, far left to right: **Easy house plants. Jade plant** (***Crassula ovata***), **peace lily** (***Spathiphyllum* spp.**), **bromeliad, chain of hearts** (***Ceropegia woodii***), **bromeliad,** ***Brighamia insignis.***
Left: **Toxin-beating spider plant** ***Chlorophytum comosum.***

Grocery-store gardening

The range of houseplants from garden centres or DIY stores can be a little boring, majoring on palms, cacti and ferns. Although I've a soft spot for many of these, I got to a point where I hankered for something different. Another problem is that decent-sized houseplants are often expensive, while cheap ones tend to give up the ghost soon after you walk them through your front door. I wanted something cheap and something that was to hand in whichever city I was living in. Like elsewhere in my life, the inspiration I needed was in the stuff that usually gets thrown out – plants I wanted were in my kitchen and compost bin.

I started with the obvious – the avocado. I love its kitsch seventies' appeal; think of Mary Ann Singleton in *Tales of the City* sprouting her lunchtime avocado at her office desk. It's a great houseplant as it doesn't mind a fair amount of neglect and rewards any love with a full flush of growth. From there I took my cupboards and fruit bowl as inspiration.

There are a few considerations to grocery-store gardening. Many modern fruit and vegetables have inhibitors to stop them germinating in storage – this is particularly true of potatoes – and it's best to go for organic produce where possible. Some stuff just doesn't

Below, left to right: **Grocery gardening. Pomegranate, chickpea, chilli plant, goji berry and ginger, all from the kitchen.**

have any seed to germinate, clearly you'll never get a banana seed. And some produce will be hybrid varieties so you might not get what you expect.

A general rule for germinating from fruit is the riper the better – even rotten – as these seeds have had time to mature. If your mango or avocado was hard, the seed probably won't be ready. If you work with the seasons, you always get better results, so start sprouting seeds in late spring and early summer and you'll have enough light to get things going.

Another rule is always to use good-quality, multi-purpose compost. If you want to be fancy, you can use stuff specially formulated for houseplants. Generally houseplants need to be kept moist, but not sodden. The rule is to water gently until it rises to the rim of the pot, not until it's sloshing all over the surface. Once the water has run right the way through the pot and collected on the saucer or plate, leave it for fifteen minutes or so. If that excess water hasn't been re-absorbed, pour it away. With heavy pots, I remove the excess water with a turkey baster.

Much grocery-store fare comes tender plants from tropical climates, but by growing them indoors you can maintain the 20-30°C that many of these plants need. Grocery-store gardening is not about trying to crop fruit because much of what you grow won't fruit till they are fully mature trees. It's about softening your environment with something green and alive.

Fruit

Papaya is easy to germinate and plants grow fast. Clean the seeds and germinate them in compost mixed with a third grit or vermiculite, sowing about 1.5cm deep. Water the compost liberally but don't completely saturate it, cover the pot with a plastic bag and leave it on a sunny windowsill. In warm bright conditions,

Left: My beautiful avocado after several years. Below: To grow your own, sprout the pip in water in a warm, dark place. Once they've got several leaves, it's time to pot them into compost.

Above left: **Chilli plant grown from seed. Most chillies are annuals and will only last a season or two.** Above right: **Sweet potatoes like lots of light and plenty of water.**

seedlings are quick to sprout. Remove the bag once seedlings have popped up and water frequently without drowning them. Repot into individual pots as soon as they are large enough to handle. Mature plants need a bright location and regular watering. If they don't get enough water, they'll drop their leaves all at once, shortly afterwards they'll droop and die. Papayas are not for the neglectful gardener, but if you love them, they'll grow as big as you let them.

Mango seed is best harvested from almost rotting fruit. Clean all the stringy bits and pulp from the seed and leave it overnight to dry. With a sharp knife, cut carefully down one side of the seed and take out the bean. Sow it flat, 2.5cm deep, and cover the pot with a plastic bag. Remove the plastic bag only when the seedling is up and standing strong, about 5cm tall. Mangoes like moist, fertile soil and sunny conditions. A regular liquid feed does them good.

Limes, lemons, oranges and grapefruit can all be grown from seed and make lovely houseplants, though they will rarely fruit indoors. Choose ripe or even slightly over-ripe fruit

and sow fresh seed in the summer in pots filled with two-thirds multi-purpose compost and one-third grit. Make sure there is a good layer of grit at the bottom for extra drainage and cover the pot with another 5mm layer of grit. Don't allow your seedlings to dry out and weed out any puny ones. Once a few are well-established, you can knock them out of the pot, carefully transplanting each one into a 9cm pot to start with. Always hold seedlings by the leaves, never handle their stems or roots. I'm afraid your plants won't flower until they are at least seven years old, but the glossy leaves smell lovely and they are handsome plants. Lemons tend to be the easiest in containers. All citrus plants need regular feeding every fortnight during summer, preferably with a specific citrus feed.

Most people know the avocado pip, toothpicks and jar of water trick from childhood. It's a bit hit-and-miss, but with patience most do sprout. There are other ways. I found in a very neglectful moment that if you just leave the whole pip covered in water in a bowl it will sprout. Once it has sprouted, you can convert to the toothpick and jar method. You can get avocados to sprout super-quickly in a worm bin, and fairly quickly in a compost bin, but it's a bit hard to find them once you've put them in! As soon as the pip has sprouted roots and a shoot, transplant into a 20cm pot. When the plant reaches 30cm tall, prune back the top third to a bud. Pomegranates can be successfully sown provided that you let the seed dry out for a few days first by spreading it on a kitchen towel. Then clean any off residue carefully and sow the seed 1.5cm deep in good, moist potting compost and cover the pot with a plastic bag. Keep it on a sunny windowsill and be patient; the seed takes up to two months to germinate before you can de-bag the pot. Don't let the compost dry out and, when seedlings appear, keep them moist. The best time to

Above left: **Sow chickpeas from your store cupboard (mine were four years out of date) in good compost.** Below left: **A young plant.** Above: **Mature plant in fruit. Sow in spring: chickpeas will have set fruit and died by autumn.**

germinate seed is late spring and early summer so pomegranates can benefit from time outside in hot summers.

Goji berries bought dried from health food stores germinate very, very quickly. It's a bit laborious cleaning the seeds from the fruit, but you do get to eat the fruit as you go. Sow them onto the surface of your compost and cover with a layer of sieved compost, grit and water. They'll take two or three weeks to

germinate; if you wait longer than four weeks they're not coming. These are tough plants – even though they're some kind of new superfood they were much loved by the Victorians and will happily grow in pots. Water them well and don't let them get too hot – a covered porch is ideal. If you can keep them somewhere bright and give them summers outside they should even fruit after three or four years.

How to rescue neglected houseplants

Problems that aren't the fault of little critters tend to come down to three things – water, light and food. You can break down people who love houseplants into over-indulgers and under-indulgers. The trick with houseplants is to be consistent. They want consistent temperature, consistent light and regular watering. Over the seasons the conditions in your home tend to vary, so move your plants around to get the best light and the warmest conditions.

The under-indulgers

Water is a prime need. The most obvious sign of a thirsty plant is when its leaves and stem start to wilt, looking soft and droopy rather than strong and healthy. This happens when the plant cells lose water and thus their turgidity (firmness). Basically the cell begins to collapse in on itself as the cell wall starts to pull away from the membrane and the plant droops. This is called 'the point of elasticity', and past that point the plant doesn't just wilt, it also starts dropping its leaves. When the membrane has literally pulled away from the cell wall through lack of water, it is no longer elastic and the leaf falls off because the cells are dead.

Other indications of a thirsty plant are if new leaves are smaller than normal and much darker coloured than others, which shows that they're in danger of dropping. Actually, plants shed older leaves first in order to save younger ones, and stunted growth often indicates underwatering and underfeeding.

Extreme dryness needs to be dealt with swiftly. Water the compost thoroughly, then soak the pot in a bowl of water for 15 minutes or until the compost is saturated. Also spray the leaves to slow down the rate of transpiration. It's hard to tell at a glance that some plants are suffering; stiff-textured leaves such as cacti or aloes can dry out with no more than a few wrinkles.

This is deceptive because they may look alive, but are mummified and actually dead. You will learn to recognise this as the leaves remain a dull green colour.

Most bought-in houseplants arrive potted in peat. This is because it's cheap and lightweight, easy to transport. Once peat has really dried out, it's difficult to re-wet. The ideal solution is to repot all your plants into something organic and peat-free, but life's a little too short to always go down that route. So if you forget to water and find a gasping houseplant, soak the whole pot in a sinkful of water and add a touch of biodegradable washing-up liquid. This breaks the surface tension of the water and, after about ten minutes, the peat should have re-absorbed.

The over-indulgers

If houseplants got obituaries you'd find the majority of them drowned. All plants take up water through very fine roots called root hairs. Clearly these like water, but they also need oxygen. If all the spaces between the particles of compost are taken up with water, there's no room for the oxygen and the plant gasps its last.

You get plenty of warnings that this is happening, but unfortunately they can also seem to point to other maladies. If the leaves wilt but the compost is wet, you're almost certainly overwatering. If they rot, or turn yellow, and flower buds fall off, too much water is the likely cause. Green slime on top of the compost is another bad sign.

It's too late to salvage a plant if the stem and lower leaves start to rot. This is a sure sign that the roots are rotten too. But it's always worth a last life-saving attempt before ditching it. First put the plant into a warm room and do not water it. Let the compost dry out and restrain yourself from watering it for at least another week to ten days. Then, and only then, you should turn the plant out of the pot and see if you can find any white, firm and healthy looking new roots. If so, well done, you've brought it back from the brink. Now you can start to water sparingly.

Light

After water comes light in the houseplant wish list. If your plants are getting too much, you may see browning at the edge of the leaves as scorching often manifests itself as brown, dead patches on leaves. Wilting, the commonest indicator of an unhappy indoor plant, can be a sign that the roots are burning to death because a pot is standing in baking sun. Feel the pot: if it's hot, so are the roots. As long as you keep giving a plant the right level of water it's hard to kill it from too much light, but it may start to look ugly. When you prune off scorched brown leaves remember that the new shoots that follow are very sensitive, so don't let them get scorched or you'll really be testing the poor plant.

Too little light can be just as bad, leading to spindly, unhappy plants. Green leaves may lose their colour and bleach to yellow, and variegated leaves may lose their variegation and turn green. Or a plant may develop contorted leaves that twist to strain towards the light. If a plant becomes truly contorted, prune it back to less twisted stems. Slowly adjust deprived plants to lighter conditions. Usually a summer outside rectifies a lot.

Food

It's probably safe to say that if you don't water enough your plants will be underfed. An underfed plant tends to look a little yellow because it is lacking essential nitrogen, the most important nutrient for a plant and essential for growth. Lack of nitrogen seriously inhibits a plant. It will grow slowly with only small, poorly coloured leaves and flowers.

During spring and summer, plants in pots need to be regularly fed. Many companies offer slow-release fertilisers that will last a season. It's a good, lazy approach, but suitable organic products are few and far between. It's best to feed your plants every two weeks with a weak liquid food such as seaweed solution. A houseplant that hasn't had its compost changed in years is at a severe disadvantage. Giving a fortnightly feed is kindness; changing the potting compost is love.

An overfed plant looks just as unhealthy, with lanky, weak growth. If your plant is in a clay pot, you may see a white, salty-looking deposit on the outside. This usually indicates mineral build-up from overfeeding. The solution is to feed sparingly, never more than fortnightly in a growing season.

Going away for the weekend?

If you're just going away for two or three days, you can seal your plants in clear plastic bags – either the whole plant or just the pot for larger plants, tying the bag securely around the stem. A bag right around the plant acts like a mini greenhouse: as the plant transpires it will release water, keeping the environment moist. A bag around the pot keeps moisture in the compost so the plant doesn't dry out. Keep the plant out of direct light, but not in a dark room. I move everything to my bathroom, that way I don't have to think about whether to keep the curtains open or closed.

If it's not practical to move your plants, use an old plastic bottle as drip irrigation. Take a bottle with a traditional screw cap and make five or so holes in it. Cut off the bottom of the bottle, turn it upside down and insert the neck end into the compost, taking care not to damage the plant's roots. Fill with water and gravity will slowly pull the water down. This method is also great for large pots and balcony planters.

How does your garden grow?

The secret to any lush, bountiful garden is good soil. Before you start gardening outside, you have to find out what type of soil you're working with, and what you're aiming for. Understanding what sort of soil you've got is akin to knowing whether your car runs on diesel or petrol. It's easy to know what you're giving your plants in a container, but there are all sorts of variations in garden soil.

Soil is your plants' source of nutrients, water and air, and it provides support and protection for their roots. Although plants make their food from the sun, water and air, they need nutrients to carry out certain functions, in just the same way that we need vitamins. Nutrients prevent stunted, slow growth and yellow, fading or unhealthy leaf colour. Plants obviously need water to stop their leaves and stems drying out, and water carries nutrients and sugars around the plant in the form of sap.

Air is as vital in the soil as it is above ground. Roots need air to breathe and they get this from tiny air pockets in the soil. Saturated or flooded soil kills plants partly because the roots are prevented from getting any air, whereas a healthy soil has space between its particles to trap air. This is one of the many reasons why organic matter is so important in soil. Where there's organic matter, there are worms and other soil organisms that live off it, and as they burrow and move around to feed, they create drainage channels, bringing much-needed air into the soil.

What is your soil type?

Soil is ancient, it was made millions upon millions of years ago, which is why it is such a precious resource. What kind of soil you have depends on the parent rock where you live. For instance you may be on chalk, which is made of trillion-year-old seashells, or on sandstone. Parent rock also determines the chemical elements found in soil and therefore how fertile it is. But soil is made up not just of ground rocks, but also organic matter. This is material made from decaying matter – animal bodies, twigs, leaves, dead plants and anything else that has fallen to the ground at some stage and decomposed.

There are three basic types of soil – clay, loam and sand. Loam is the most desirable as it's a balanced mix of the three. Clay and sand are less ideal, but you can gradually work them to make them more like loam. In many urban areas you find soil that behaves a bit like sand, but is actually more rubble than anything else.

Clay soil is made up of very fine particles that bind tightly together. This is why it turns sticky after the rain. Once it dries, it sets like concrete and cracks. Clay soils tend to have an orange tinge.

Sandy soil is made up of fine particles of sand and grit, which makes it very free draining. Sandy soils tend to be pale, sometimes with a pinkish tinge. They are often lacking organic matter.

Loam soils are made up of equal parts of sand, clay and loam. They are typically dark brown because they contain plenty of organic matter.

Some experts recommend doing a soil analysis test to tell you what type of soil you're working with, including its pH and mineral content. This is done either by buying a soil-testing kit from the garden centre – generally worthless in my opinion – or sending it off to a soil-testing laboratory. A lab report can be very useful, but it has to be thorough to be worthwhile and it's not cheap. I admit that I don't bother as you can tell an awful lot by digging up some soil and rolling it around in your hands.

You can also tell a lot about your own soil by looking in your neighbours' gardens. If you spot lots of drought-loving plants, you probably have thin, well-drained soil. If there are lots of damp-loving plants such as hostas, giant rhubarbs and giant cowslips, your soil is probably fairly dense and boggy. Or you could just ask your neighbours; they may be the sort who sent their soil off to a lab. Your local garden centre is sure to know the general local conditions, although they might try and sell you a kit to see for yourself.

The hand test

Take a small handful of wet soil and roll it between your palms. If it makes a snake that can be bent into a circle without breaking, it's clay. If it makes a snake, but crumbles when you bend it, you have loam. If it's too crumbly to roll into a snake, it's either sand, which is usually pale brown, or made up of rubble, brick dust and all the other stuff buried in urban back gardens.

Soil structure

A good soil structure contains particles of various sizes with different-sized gaps and spaces between them which hold their shape under slight pressure. Different types of soil have different structures: the best are full of organic matter and the poorest can be improved by regularly adding organic matter in the form of composts and manures.

The way to tell what you're working with is simple. Take a small handful of soil and rub it between your thumb and forefinger. If it feels gritty it contains a lot of sand, if it feels smooth it contains a good proportion of silt (an important component of loam soils), and if it feels sticky and has a sheen, it's clay.

Clay soils

Heavy clay tends to become compacted and airless and is very low in organic matter. Clay drains badly; in summer it can dry out to become as hard as concrete, in winter it often becomes waterlogged. This means that through the winter plant roots too often drown as they are starved of oxygen. On really heavy clay, plants can only grow roots in a very shallow surface area. This means that come summer, when the surface of clay bakes dry, plants don't have enough root depth to extract water from lower down. On exposed sites, plants dry out particularly fast in summer months.

Clay is sticky and compacts very easily, especially where there is a lot of footfall. For this reason, it's best to try to keep off beds in wet weather, and it's never a good plan to try and cultivate a clay soil when it's soggy. Clay is also slow to warm up in spring, but you can help it along for spring sowing by covering beds with carpet, fleece or clear plastic.

But clay soils hold nutrients well because they don't drain away, so you won't have to feed your plants as often as you would in other soils.

Management On heavy clay, you will have to add a bucketful of grit per square metre to open up the soil. Horticultural grit is very expensive as it has been washed and graded; sharp sand is cheaper and can be mixed in equal parts with grit to make your money go further. Don't use builder's sand as it's full of lime, and don't use sea gravel as it's too salty. Every three years, you should also try to add at least a bucketful of home-made or bought compost per square metre – organic, peat-free soil improver or multi-purpose compost is best. By digging this in, you improve the structure to make it looser and less liable to compact.

If your soil is really heavy and your time limited, it may be a better plan to create raised beds on top of the soil and fill them with compost – again use a mix of multi-purpose compost and peat-free soil improver, ideally with some home-made compost mixed in. If they're available, you could also combine good topsoil and possibly a bit of farmyard manure.

Choose plants for clay carefully. Most herbaceous perennials will have no problem once they're established but some plants, including penstemons, lavenders and rosemary, don't like sitting with wet feet.

Sandy soils

Sandy or gravelly soils are thin and rapidly dry out in both summer and winter because drainage can be almost too good. They don't hold nutrients well as they drain away swiftly, so plants on sandy soils will need feeding regularly. If sandy soil is left bare for any period, it is quick to erode.

Management If you want to grow vegetables in sandy soil (apart from carrots that prefer it), the only real solution is to add bucketloads of compost to bulk out the organic matter and thus improve the water-holding

capacity. If you can't dig, then mulch heavily (covering the soil with a thick layer of organic matter, such as manure or compost). Whether you dig or mulch, do it regularly in both spring and autumn. These are hungry, fast-draining soils that will literally eat up organic matter.

Stick to a base of Mediterranean and drought-loving plants such as rock roses (*Cistus*), thyme (*Lavatera*), yarrows (*Achillea*) and lavenders (*Lavendula*). This will cut down your labour because these plants are perfectly suited to dry, hot, free-draining conditions. Many poor urban soils behave like sandy soil.

Loam

Loam, lovely loam is naturally full of organic matter and therefore worms, soil organisms and life. Full of

Above: Mediterranean plants such as thyme (here with a chive in flower) thrive in free-draining conditions such as sandy or urban soils.

nutrients, it is moist but free-draining, the perfect garden soil. Whereas clay will be covered in puddles for ages after heavy rain, puddles on loam soils won't last more than an hour or two, yet in summer whatever moisture is available will be held and well distributed in a loam soil.

Management Loam starts life with a fair amount of organic matter, but don't abuse its good nature. If you grow lots of vegetables and flowers, you should keep adding more compost and give it a thorough feed every two or three years.

Soil health checks

Above: **Good soil is teeming with life. Look for worms, beetles, woodlice and mites as a sign of healthy soil fauna.**

Once you've assessed your soil type and structure, check a few more things to see just how healthy your soil is. The first is organic matter. You'll get a rough idea of how much you've got in your soil by digging up a spadeful and counting the worms. Conventional wisdom says dig a spit – a spade's blade depth – deep. Three worms are good, five worms are excellent, no worms are bad. Dig in several places and if you can't find worms your soil is very low in organic matter.

You can also count other soil dwellers in your spadeful of soil. You might have to wait a little while to see anything, as tiny soil creatures can be hard to spot, but good soil will be alive with activity. As well as earth worms, you may see little things hopping and jumping, beetles, woodlice and fine white threads of fungi. Soil organisms are the source of life in your garden: they break down decaying matter, make nutrients available to plants and create channels for water to move through. If you can count more than ten living things in your soil you've got a really good starting point.

Don't worry if you've scored poorly; many of us are working with problematic soils. Most urban dwellers are lumbered with clay or thin or gritty soil so low in organic matter it's a surprise even the weeds grow. All soil can be transformed into a healthy growing medium, and it does not have to be done all at once.

It's also helpful to assess how compacted your soil is. Get a long piece of thin, straight wire and prod it into the ground. At the point where the wire bends you've hit compaction, so if it bends near the surface you have very compacted soil. The wire could be hitting a stone, so try a few times in different spots. If you hit a line of solid spots, you've got what's known as a 'pan' – a layer of compacted soil that limits root growth. You get a pan if heavy machinery has been working over your soil – most often on new building developments. A pan can be rock hard, so it must be broken up before you start planting.

Soil pH

How acid or alkaline your soil is determined by its pH; pH is measured on a scale of 1 (very acid) to 14 (very alkaline). Most soils fall between 6–8, either slightly acid or alkaline, and for most plants that's just fine. The problem is with the extremes. Very acid or very alkaline soils have problems with certain nutrients, which become chemically locked up in the soil and thus unavailable to the plants. When this happens, you see deficiencies. On alkaline soil, you tend to get iron and some trace elements locked up. This is why, if you grow acid lovers such as rhododendrons on alkaline soil, their leaves turn yellow – a sure sign of iron deficiency.

Many plants, especially vegetables such as the cabbage family (*Brassica*), like slightly alkaline conditions where nutrients are readily available to them. Acid soils tend to lock up phosphates: if your plants have stunted growth and purple-tinged leaves they're missing phosphates. Acid-loving plants have overcome these problems, but can be unwilling to grow in anything other than acid soils for this reason.

Altering the pH

Most soils sit somewhere near the neutral pH line, which is where most plants want to be. If yours is very acid or alkaline, this does determine your choices but on the whole I tend not to modify neutral soil for acid or alkaline lovers as long as their other needs are met. If they're kept moist in summer and well drained in winter, most will survive, even if the pH is not perfect.

It is possible to alter the pH, but it tends to be only a temporary solution – you couldn't change the pH in a whole garden, it would just be too difficult. You can however raise the pH of an acid soil by adding lime. Lime supplies calcium to the soil. Earthworms, soil organisms and nitrogen-fixing bacteria all increase their activity in alkaline soils for this reason. Lime doesn't last in the soil that long, so you will have to regularly test your soil, year on year. It is important not to put lime and organic matter on your soil at the same time as they will react together and cancel the effect.

You'll get a big hint if your garden is acid or alkaline if it's full of certain plants, or if they are flourishing next door. Thriving rhododendrons, azaleas, heathers and conifers suggest an acid soil. Pinks and carnations, lilacs, scabious and the strawberry tree (*Arbutus unedo*) prefer an alkaline environment as they are chalk soil natives.

If you want to grow acid-loving plants and you have very alkaline soil, grow the plants in pots of lime-free (ericaceous) potting compost. I'll warn you now that it is very hard to find peat-free alternatives.

Make your own pH test

To check your soil pH, you can buy a kit from the garden centre, but the easiest way is to make one yourself, using red cabbage. This contains a water-soluble pigment, called a flavin, that turns red in acid conditions, has a purplish tinge in neutral conditions, and shows bluish green to greenish yellow in alkaline conditions.

Bring two cups of chopped red cabbage to the boil and let them cool. Drain off the water – and eat the cabbage! Put about a tablespoon of soil in a cup and half-fill this with water. Stir the soil around so that it's suspended in the water. Now add about 3mm of cabbage water.

The liquid will turn a purplish red with a slight tinge of blue for a neutral soil. Greenish-yellow is very alkaline and very red is acid. You should check soil at various locations around your garden. Be aware that builder's rubble contains a lot of lime which will give alkaline results, so make sure you take a few different readings.

Compost: feeding your soil for free

Most gardens do not start life with good soil. It is something that is worked at, maintained and loved. Luckily the way to a successful romance is simple, all that good soil needs is good compost.

Compost is a confusing term as it is used both for manufactured and home-made stuff and they are very different things. Shop-bought stuff is usually a blend of biodegradable material, everything from peat or shredded pallets to farmyard manure. Home-made compost is very different because you make it yourself. It is very variable, depending on what has gone on your compost heap and the composting conditions. It is very nutritious and, best of all, it's free.

Your own compost is truly the best thing for your garden. It's made from things you would otherwise either throw away or let someone else deal with – food scraps, grass cuttings, clippings, weeds, even old woollen and cotton clothes and cardboard. This waste is the source of your rich garden.

Making compost

The simplest way to make compost is to copy the forest floor. The waste that accumulates there is a mixture of animal and vegetable matter – leaves, twigs, branches, fruit, seeds, conifer needles, insect and mammal poop and eventually their bodies. All this is washed and sieved by rain, sifted through by yet more insects and bacteria and, with time, nature turns it all into the finest-quality soil. So if you were to gather all your leaves, clippings, weeds and food scraps into a heap and leave it for a year or so you too would have some fine soil. But a year is a long time to wait and not many people are too keen on a scrappy pile in their garden, so most of us choose to use a compost bin. There's sure to be one to meet your particular space and style needs.

There are two myths about compost that seem to stop people becoming master composters. Myth number one is that compost smells bad. Emphatically not true. Good compost smells rich and healthy. Myth number two is that good compost takes years to make. Rubbish. Good compost can be made in around four months in the summer; over the winter it will take up to twice that long.

Making compost is just like baking a cake or making bread. You have to put in the right ingredients and mix them together in vaguely the right amounts. If you put only grass clippings in your pile, it won't rot down for a very long time but will just turn into a slimy green mess. If all you try to compost are great chunks of branches or roots, these will take years to rot down. The key is to create a balance between the brown stuff you put on, and the green stuff – otherwise known as the carbon/nitrogen ratio. You should have about two-thirds brown stuff (carbon source) to one-third green (nitrogen). Brown broadly represents carbon found in fibrous material such as twigs and stems, straw, cardboard and roots. Green refers to nitrogen found in plant leaves, stems, grass, flowers and weeds.

Chop up your branches, throw on all your vegetable scraps and annual weeds, add a few thin layers of grass clippings (never more than 15cm deep). Hurl on a pizza box, rip up your old cotton jeans, add some plant prunings, and mix. That's all there is to it. You'll end up with a delicious rich dark crumbly cake. All you have to do is spread this across the top of your garden and the worms will dig it in for you. The sum total of your expenditure will have been to walk to your compost bin a few times a week with vegetable scraps, to turn your compost once or twice and then to spread it.

I like to collect my vegetable scraps in the kitchen so I don't have to be constantly walking back and

Above left: **Compost crocks – I found this chicken in a skip. She conveniently holds a week's worth of peeling.** Above right: **Turning your compost regularly speeds things up no end.**

forth to the compost. You can buy specially designed compost caddies with filters to stop them smelling. I had one for a while, but I tended to become very lazy and as it didn't smell I let it sit, cramming more and more waste in, until it became an exploding mass of fruit flies. Now I use a lovely white ceramic chicken that I found in a skip. The lid keeps the flies out and it holds just enough for a week's worth of peelings.

Compost ingredients are chiefly broken down by aerobic bacteria. In order to do this fast and efficiently they need plenty of air and moisture. The faster the bacteria work, the hotter the conditions get. Cooking the compost is fairly essential as it kills off weed seeds, pathogens and plant diseases. A large compost heap,

anything a metre wide or more, will easily reach 60–70°C in a matter of hours. A small pile will bake much more gently and perhaps never reach quite the same temperature, which is one of its limitations.

However, you can help the bacteria by having some sort of bin for your compost, to insulate the pile and provide the right conditions for the 'bacterial bonfire'. Think of building your compost a little like a bonfire. Air needs to be drawn from the bottom up through

Compost tips

Start your compost from someone else's. Get a friend with good compost to give you a bagful as a starter. It will contain all sorts of bacteria, insects, worms and good composting things.

Never try to make compost from one ingredient.

Make your compost in layers, 15–25cm deep.

Mix your compost at least once every six weeks.

Branches or roots take a long time to decompose; chop them into roughly 20cm-long pieces.

Thin cardboard, shredded paper and scrunched-up newspaper are excellent sources of carbon. Highly coloured, glossy paper contains too many chemicals and will upset the worms. Remember this mantra '*Vogue* bad, *Private Eye* good'.

Dog and cat poop are bad news and must never be put in the compost.

Pigeon poop is great and speeds things up.

Never put meat, fish or dairy to compost.

Tea bags, coffee grounds and vacuum-cleaner waste can all go in.

Wood or bonfire ash is good, coal ash is bad.

Don't put perennial weeds straight onto the compost. Put these into a bucket of water and cover for around three weeks. This allows them to rot. Then pour this liquid mix onto the compost. This way you get all the nutrients without the risk of infestation.

Don't put diseased plants into your compost. Your compost isn't sterile and you'll re-introduce the disease back into your garden.

Go easy on the lemon peel. Too much citrus can rock the balance and upset the worms.

Right: **Brown stuff. Chop up large roots or branches, otherwise they'll take forever to break down. Branches are high in carbon, so if you add a lot you'll need a source of nitrogen, such as weeds.**

the centre of the heap to get the bonfire going. One way to do this, particularly if your bin is plastic, is to lay several bricks on their edges at the bottom of the bin. This creates a layer on which the compost will sit, drawing air from below. It's always a good idea to have a lid for your bin to keep the rain out and the heat in, but make sure that it lets air through. If it's a plastic lid, I'd make some small holes in it to draw air out.

Compost also needs moisture. If it's too dry, the compost will virtually stand still, but if it's too wet, especially if this is coupled with too little air, you'll get anaerobic conditions and the pile will start to produce methane. This is a big no no, since the planet doesn't need any more. If you use a plastic bin, you'll have to be more careful not to create these conditions or you'll get a slimy, rotting, very smelly mess.

If you get into composting in a big way you don't have to be limited by your own biodegradable waste. You can find lots of places to get waste for free – people will even be pleased for you to take it away. Most coffee shops have loads of used grounds which they chuck away – it's a perfect compost material. Pet shops that sell birds have lots of poop and nothing to do with it. Local pubs and restaurants will have vegetable scraps, and work canteens will be pleased for you to take home their used teabags. You may have to provide containers and promise regular collection, but it's worth it.

Composting is the ultimate in low-key recycling, with no miles, little processing and no packaging. And even if you neglect your pile of waste, with time nature will turn it into compost, the best and cheapest soil improver you will ever have.

Rodents

Your compost heap is a unique wildlife habitat, home to hundreds of tiny creatures and a wonderful foraging opportunity for lots more. But occasionally you may have unwanted visitors such as mice or rats. They are actually pretty easy to get rid of. Mice can be a real nuisance in the garden, they love many seeds and are particularly partial to peas, beans and tulip bulbs. Rats don't do much harm, but they are unpleasant and no one wants to meet one when dropping off their scraps.

There are three important things to know about the common rat. It is commensal, meaning it lives primarily by eating our food. It is neophobic, which means it is very wary of new things. It is thigmophilic, meaning it relies principally on touch to navigate. If you never turn your compost bin you unwittingly create a very comfortable rat home – an unchanging shelter full of food to burrow into. But the more you turn the compost, the less a rat will want to visit, because if it is a changing environment, rats won't create runs and certainly won't nest there.

Rats have certain food preferences and if you have or fear a rat problem it might be wise to stay clear of eggs or wash eggshells before you put them on the compost. Also avoid bananas and melon rind and be doubly careful not to put cooked scraps or bread into your heap. You can put all these into a worm compost bin instead.

Mice may nest in the compost during the winter when it's warm – turning the compost is the quickest way to discourage them. If you find toads or frogs in your compost, award yourself a gold medal. It's a sign that your compost is definitely alive and healthy.

Build your own compost bin

The bin is loosely designed around a beehive, a simple design of stacking boxes with a pitched roof. I designed it to make it easy to turn the compost and speed the process. Once the bin is full you remove the roof, carefully take off the first box and place it beside your (now shorter) bin. This becomes the new base. You turn the exposed compost into this new base, then take off the next box and stack it on the first, and follow the same process for all three. It can be a little messy, but once you've done it once or twice you'll find you can flip the whole lot in no time. The more you flip, the more the compost will break down. The quicker it breaks down, the quicker it shrinks, so a full bin one week will have space for more compost the next.

My compost bin is built entirely of reclaimed wood. To make it more attractive, I hunted high and low for substantial Georgian skirting boards, but it could be made out of virtually any wood, except chipboard. Chipboard is the Weetabix of the wood world, when it gets wet it turns to mush and is totally unsuitable for living outside. I also used old pine floorboards, equally good would be timber from pallets, staircases or shelves. In my neck of the woods, there is so much renovation going on that skirting board hits the skips daily, but if your local skips offer only rubble and rubbish you'll have to buy the wood. Always ask for wood approved by the FSC.

To make the bin, you need an electric or hand drill with a 3mm wood drill bit. You will save your wrists and time if you have a screwdriver head on your drill. I painted the entire box with primer paint before finishing it off with blackboard paint because I wanted the bin to look good and to extend its life. It's made from wood that was never intended to live outside, so the paint will protect it from the worst of the weather. The blackboard paint means you can draw on it, which is useful for first-time composters as you can mark the date of your first filling and know how long it's been in there.

Materials

21 boards of equal length: 60cm makes an effective small box, 80cm is ideal for a larger space.

18 battens of a length equal to the width of boards

36 x 20mm wood screws

1 tin of external timber paint or stain if using untreated wood

Blackboard paint (optional)

Wood saw

Electric drill with 3mm wood bit and Philips screwdriver head

2 G-clamps and a workbench are useful. If you don't have these, you'll need a spare pair of hands at some point.

To create the boxes

If the wood has come from a skip, it may need cleaning up. Remove any old nails or screws and sand off any plaster, glue or other material. Cut the wood into equal lengths: 60cm makes a good smaller-sized composter – I wouldn't go longer than 80cm. All your boards need to be the same length, but each layer can be a different height, so you can use up whatever width of wood you can find.

1. You will need to make three boxes. Each corner needs to be a proper right angle, so place each board flat on the ground and secure a batten to one end.

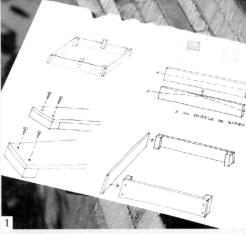

2. You need to place a batten at one end of each board, making sure the edges are flush. Pre-drill guide holes through the whole lot and then screw the battens to the boards.

3. Then fit four boards together to make a box. It's easiest if you clamp the boards together before you drill. If you don't have a clamp, a spare pair of hands is useful. Make sure all the ends are flush. Some people find it easier to attach battens to both ends of two boards, then screw the other two unbattened boards onto these.

Repeat to make three boxes.

On two sides of each box you need to screw a batten, roughly 12cm long, inside the top edge to keep the boxes firmly stacked. The battens should stand 6cm above the top edge of each box. Fix each batten with two screws, drilling from the outside of the board. The battens don't have to be in the same place on each box.

The roof

A roof is a good idea on a compost bin as it will stop nutrients being washed away by the rain and also help keep heat in during the winter. It isn't essential though – you could put carpet on top of the bin in winter instead – but a roof looks more attractive. You'll need nine boards, cut to the same length as your box

sides, three for the sides and six to cover the roof. I used skirting board again.

4. Take three of your pieces of board. Cut one board in half lengthways. This will make the sides of the roof. On the other two boards, draw a line halfway, but don't cut. Find the middle point of each piece and draw a diagonal line from this to the half height mark at both ends of each board. This should give you a pitch. Cut along the diagonal lines on both boards. Join the four sides together with battens flush to the ends.

5. You will need six pieces to cover the roof, laid horizontally, overlapping to form a slope. Lay the bottom two boards first, these should overhang the edge slightly for water run-off. Screw these in place. Follow these with the middle two and screw them down.

6. The final two boards need to be placed so that there is a gap of about 5cm at the top to let small amounts of rainwater in and air out of the compost. You now have a pitched roof.

On the inside of the roof, attach two bits of wood (offcuts are ideal) to the back wall. These will act as hinges and stop the roof from falling off when you lift it up.

You can attach a prop on the inside of the roof to keep the roof open while you throw in your peelings. This should be roughly 60mm long. Use a screw to attach one end, making sure that it is loose enough for you to swivel the prop. On the other end of the prop, cut a small groove to rest on the edge of the box. You may want to hammer a nail to the inside of the lid to hook the prop onto, so it doesn't fall down each time you open the lid.

If you are composting on a deck, you could make a large tray for the box to sit on. The tray will have to be twice the size of the box so you can still turn it.

4

5

6

Using your compost

I cannot bang on enough about how good home-made compost is for soil. It's simply the best stuff you'll ever get hold of for free. Dig it in to see immediate improvements, or spread it thickly as a layer of mulch to keep down weeds and let the worms take it into the soil. You can also use it as a base for your own potting compost mix.

If home-made compost is destined for seed sowing, it has to be mixed with other ingredients. You never use it straight, it's just too rich in nutrients for baby plants – it would be a bit like starting them on steroids. Another thing to remember is that it hasn't been sterilised like bought-in composts, so if you use it as a sowing base, there's a good chance that some of your seedlings may be weeds.

It is satisfying to have your own compost for sowing seeds, but once you start making compost you'll find you will rarely have enough. If you use it as a regular soil conditioner and mulch, and add a layer to feed your containers, you rarely have any spare to make your own potting mixtures. You need to decide where it's needed most. In my garden, my thin, urban soil is crying out for richness and all my compost goes back into it. When I need seed or container compost, I buy British peat-free stuff from a store, and all the hard work is done for me. But if your garden consists of a few window boxes or containers on a deck or a patio, then blending your own home-made stuff clearly makes sense.

The basic mix for seed compost is two parts of home-made compost – sieve any big lumps through some kind of mesh or old wire basket – to one part loam (which you'll probably have to buy), one part bought bark or home-made leaf mould, and one part sand.

Above: **Add home-made compost to holes before planting shrubs or roses to give them a head start in life.**

Worm composting

Worm composting is the new cool because you don't even have to have an outdoor space to compost. Recycling is good ecology and economy, and the very best environmentalism starts and finishes at home. This is why having a compost bin is vital and if it's a compost bin filled with lots of bits from stuff you grew and ate, that's even better. It is a really appropriate use of energy, and an independent one. However, many of us don't have the space for conventional composting, so that's where the worms come in.

A worm bin is basically a composting system where the chief composters are worms. You naturally find worms in compost and this system exploits that so that you can make compost in a very small space.

Worm-bin style

You can buy very good worm bins online. These range from a simple box or plastic bins to a stacking can called a Can o' worms, where the worms eat one layer of food, and then move up to the next, making harvesting the compost very easy. These tend to be fairly costly, but you can make your own from wood or plastic. I made a wooden one because it was easier to find the materials for free.

The minimum size usually recommended for a worm bin is 30 x 60 x 90cm, but mine measures 20 x 40 x 60cm. With a squeeze, it can live under my sink in winter – it seems to work just fine. The size of a bin does depend how much waste you produce. If you don't produce much or you're using it as a secondary compost system, you can get away with the slightly smaller bin.

There are dozens of designs on the web for DIY boxes as well as boxes to buy. But if you want a very simple one that works, try copying mine – it's just a lidded wooden box with holes drilled into the sides.

Wooden bins breathe better than plastic ones, but deteriorate quicker as the wood is permanently damp. Plastic ones need more holes to breathe and they accumulate more liquid. In some systems, this is collected and drained through a spigot to produce worm tea, a delicious and nutritious brew for your plants. You'll need to dilute worm tea though, as it's really potent stuff – dilute by a third.

My worm box

I started with a really sturdy box that I found in a skip, but of course you could start by building a box from scratch using boards 2.5cm thick.

Materials

2 pieces of board (30 x 90cm) for the front and back

2 pieces (30 x 60cm) for the sides

1 piece of board, 60 x 90cm, for the base

32 x 35mm screws

To build the worm box

Pre-drill three guide holes 10mm in from the ends of the front and back pieces, with the top one about 2.5cm from the top edge. Pre-drill six holes 10mm in along the long edges of the base, four along the shorter edges. Using the pre-drilled holes as guides, screw the front and back pieces to the sides. Screw the bottom pieces on.

Once you have a box, you need to drill large aeration holes. You'll need a single row of six 25mm in diameter holes along the front, near the bottom edge, and a single row of holes along the back nearer to the top of the box. These allow the air to escape if the bin is too hot.

Next you need to staple or nail a screen over the holes. The screen needs to be made out of something non-biodegradable and you'll need to be inventive. I asked my ironmongers and they gave me some metal screening that I couldn't even start to tell you what it was used for. You could use any fine mesh, such as a well-cleaned old fireguard from a skip. It stops both debris and worms falling out.

Finally make a lid. This could be a single piece of plywood or lengths of plank nailed together. To make a lid for the 30 x 60 x 90cm bin from planks, you need a plank of wood 20cm wide and 3m long. Cut the wood into three pieces 90cm long and two pieces 60cm long. Lay the three 90cm pieces next to each other horizontally and then lay the two 60cm pieces vertically over them. Nail or screw the 60cm pieces to the 90cm ones and you should have a lid. Now hinge the lid to the box with

two flush hinges – 50mm work best. They must be flush hinges in order for the lid to fit snugly. My own box is hinged with some fittings rescued from an old wardrobe.

You need to raise the bin off the ground so that it doesn't rot. I used bricks, but you could screw some battens to the bottom. I painted the outside of the bin with a stain and garden furniture preservative. Never use stains or preservatives on the inside of a worm box as worms are sensitive to chemicals.

I use a bit of copper pipe as a prop to keep the lid open when I do maintenance. I guess if I'd thought harder, I might have incorporated a prop into the lid.

So there it is: a box with some holes in it, made out of wood, with a lid. Not exactly complicated. Next you need to make bedding and buy some worms.

How a worm bin works

The worms eat your leftover scraps and peelings, and they also eat the bacteria, moulds and fungi that break down the waste. Basically they consume decaying organic matter in very large quantities. Digestive enzymes in their stomachs break down the food and remove the nutrients. What is left is a mixture of soil, bacteria and plant residue, and they poop this out in the form of worm casts. It is these worm casts that you will harvest.

Worms need bedding as well as food. Their food is your waste and their bedding doesn't just make life nicer for them, it also acts as somewhere for them to lay their eggs. Worms are such good house-cleaners that at a certain point they'll eat their bedding, so you have to replenish it every three or four months.

The worms

You cannot dig up worms from a garden and put them in a worm bin. This won't work. Garden worms are soil-dwelling species. They don't process large amounts of compost, they hate confinement and they don't like being disturbed. Rather, you need composting worms that are usually red, characteristically wiggle a lot and are often called brandling worms, or tiger worms from the genus *Eisenia* or *Lumbricus*. You may be able to get hold of some from a friend, or from fishing-tackle shops, mail-order catalogues or online.

Worms are sold by weight rather than number. You need a 2:1 ratio of worms to food. One way to work out how many you need is to weigh your weekly scraps. If you have one kilo of waste, you need two kilos of worms. If you're prepared to be patient, you can get away with fewer and let them breed, but you can't add all your weekly waste or you'll overwhelm the system.

Worm bedding

Worm bedding holds moisture, provides a working environment for the worms, somewhere for you to place the waste, and ultimately becomes food for the worms. It's a source of carbon for them, so it's best to make it from a mix of several ingredients, including newspaper, coconut fibre (coir), soil, animal manure, leaf mould, wood chips or shredded documents. Or you can buy it ready made.

Moistened bedding needs to fill three-quarters of your box. The easiest base is newspaper, torn into roughly 2.5cm strips. Stick to black and white print because coloured ink is full of chemicals. Shredded documents and records are fine, but the paper is a lot harder to moisten than newspaper print. I find a coir block first soaked in hot water works well. Admittedly this isn't free, but it's clean, odourless and retains moisture really well.

To your base material you need to add a couple of trowels of garden soil for grit. Worms ingest grit and then use it to break down food particles. It's their version of teeth, I guess. Soil also adds bacteria and fungi to help the composting process. To your base of paper/coir/leaf mould/wood chips or whatever you've decided to use, add the garden soil and thoroughly mix everything together.

Opposite page, top left: **Make worm bedding by mixing shredded newspaper, coir, soil and water.** Bottom left: **Getting their new home ready.** Right: **My new friends, worms from the fishing shop.**

Worm food

Good

Vegetable peelings – go easy on the onions

Cooked vegetables

Pizza crust

Vegetarian leftovers

Tea bags

Bread

Cake

Biscuits

Baked beans

Pasta

Lettuce

Oatmeal

Pineapple rind

Any green veg or veg tops

Apple cores

Coffee grounds

Banana skins

Bad

Chillies

Hot curry leftovers

Corn on the cob husks

Fish/meat scraps – worms will clean bones, but meat makes the bin smell

Pet poop

Too much citrus as it contains limonene, which is toxic to worms.

Maintaining your worms

An hour or two after you've put your worms in their bedding, you can start adding their food – your waste. I add the food wrapped in newspaper for two reasons: it helps to keep fruit flies down (at some point all worm bins will get fruit flies) and it constantly adds more of the carbon that worms need. It also means I can see when the worms are getting into the food, so I can work out whether I'm overfeeding them.

I bury the food in a different spot each time I provide their weekly feed, trying roughly to rotate around the area. Your worm bin should be moist to the touch, not soaking and not bone dry. If the bin gets too dry, I water it a little. If it gets too wet, I add toilet roll tubes to absorb the water.

Worms don't like food that is over-spicy, salty, acidic or too large to chew. If you treat their diet a bit like feeding a toddler, you can't really go far wrong. They like a fairly bland diet – and remember they've got tiny mouths, so they can only eat tiny things or things soft enough to burrow into. Worms also need extra calcium and you can buy them calcium treats online, but eggshells are just as good so long as you pulverise them first.

Ideal worm home

Your needs and the worms' needs can happily coexist somewhere in your home. Worms convert waste at 15–25°C. They can still work at 10°C, but once you get below freezing point you start to dice with death. At low temperatures, the worms just stop working, so if you want to work them all year you need to give them the right temperature. If you want to keep your worms outside, you might have to make the box a winter coat to keep them going. Bubble wrap or polystyrene packing from around a fridge or cooker is ideal – or bring them inside. Worms also need lots of air, moisture and quite a neutral pH. A well-designed home should offer enough air, but keeping the box in a very small, stuffy place won't help. The pH is best determined by the food you give them, so make sure you don't put too many onions or orange peel in at once.

The best location for your worm bin has to be near the kitchen waste, that way you'll make sure you keep feeding them all your scraps.

Harvesting the compost

How often you harvest depends on several factors: chiefly how many worms, how often you put food in, and the temperature at which the bin is kept. During the winter, in weather below 10°C, the worms don't do much, so if you keep putting in food the system will slow down. However, in the summer you'll be able to harvest every 2–3 months. Initially you'll have to keep looking to find your pattern.

The compost is ready when it is a rich dark colour. It basically looks like a very dense, rich potting compost, and can be harvested in several ways. The laziest method is to do absolutely nothing until the whole bin has turned into very fine worm casts – say you feed them for four months over the winter and leave them for four months – but this also means you'll probably kill your worms as they run out of food and start eating their own worm casts. It also means slightly less rich compost. A better way is to divide and sort. Once the bedding has diminished to the point where there's nowhere left to bury fresh waste, it's time to add more. Push all this good compost to one side and add fresh bedding to the other side. Bury your waste in the new bedding and after a week or so the worms will have moved over so you can harvest the good stuff. Do this every two or three months to keep the system going strong.

A third method is to divide and dump. Here you take out two thirds of the compost and add fresh bedding to the remaining third, which will have enough worms and cocoons left in to keep things going. This is the most low-key method, and you may need to buy a few new worms now and again if activity looks as if it has slowed down too much.

Using worm compost

Worm compost, known as vermicompost, is superb stuff. It's particularly valuable to top-dress houseplants, adding more material and feeding them richly at the same time. If you want to sterilise the compost first to use it on houseplants, you'll need to remove any little hopping springtails. Place the compost between two sheets of plastic and leave it in the sun for a while.

Vermicompost is a prized additive to any potting compost. Add one part worm castings to four parts multi-purpose compost to add nutrients to the mix. When you're planting out seedlings, they'll be all the happier for a generous sprinkling of worm castings in the planting holes. Or scatter worm castings into the bottom of seed rows, giving the plants a rich source of nutrition to draw on soon after they germinate.

Other home-made composts

Leaf mould is another sort of compost, made entirely out of leaves. Leaf mould is nature's best seed compost as it has an open structure and holds moisture well. It's not much good on its own for mature plants since it doesn't contain much nutrition, but is best as a soil conditioner, a nutritious mulch or as an additive to bought compost for added structure.

Leaves don't decompose in the same way as garden compost, so don't put them straight onto your compost heap – they'll take much longer to break down than other materials. While regular compost uses bacteria to decompose, leaf mould needs fungi which takes longer. The best way to make leaf mould is to gather all your leaves, or get them from the street, push them into a bin bag in which you've punctured some holes, tying the bag at the neck, and let them slowly rot down. I like to put the date on to see how long it takes, and this stops it being mistaken for rubbish and thrown out.

If you've got a large garden or an allotment, it's easy to make a simple cage out of chicken wire – then you can make mountains of the stuff. If you're dealing with loads of leaves and you have a lawn mower, try mowing your leaves before you bag them. Breaking them up speeds the process of decomposition no end. I've made leaf mould in under eight months using this method. Otherwise it takes at least a year.

Pine needles are a good source for making ericaceous compost for acid-loving plants. Let them compost for a year or two, they're slow to break down. Evergreen leaves take even longer than deciduous to break down – at least two years – so it's best not to mix the two types together.

Green manures
Sometimes called cover crops, green manures are crops sown to cover an area that you can't use yet while adding fertility to it. They're most useful for allotments and some newly established gardens as they rapidly establish themselves and out-compete weeds. Once they have done their job, you dig them into the ground to increase the organic matter in the soil and act as natural fertiliser. Green manures are also an excellent vegetarian substitute to animal manures, which are good for the soil but almost impossible for urban gardeners to get in reasonable quantities.

If it looks as though you're going to have a vacant patch of soil for even a few weeks it's worth sowing a green manure. There are three forms: quick-growing leafy types, those from the pea family, and those with deep fibrous roots. Blue-flowered *Phacelia tanacetifolia* is the prettiest of the bunch. It can be used as a short-term crop that is dug in a few weeks to a couple of months later, or it can be left to flower. It took me almost a year to get round to digging one patch, but I didn't mind as it made a lovely blue carpet and the bees go wild for it. *Phacelia* can be used either as a short-term leafy crop to increase available nitrogen or as a longer-term crop so its fibrous root system can break up the soil, and it will add organic matter when dug in.

Grazing rye (*Secale cereale*) and red clover (*Trifolium pratense*) are other useful cover crops. Grazing rye has deep fibrous roots to break up the soil, but you can't sow anything else until three weeks after you've dug it in. Red clover is in the pea family and, in common with all its family members, it has nodules on its roots which fix atmospheric nitrogen. Once dug in, this is released slowly to the crops that follow it. Red clover can be used over the winter so that your ground is fertile in time for spring sowing. It's also pretty in flower.

Left: Collecting autumn leaves to make leaf mould. This takes about a year. Below: The end result – a dark brown crumbling mass ready for seed compost.

Sowing growing & protecting

Seed sowing

The building blocks of any thrifty gardener's paradise are seeds, tiny packages of promise that are sometimes free and nearly always cheap. Once you have mastered seed sowing, the world of gardening shifts a little and you'll soon realise how easy it is to create your own piece of heaven for almost nothing.

Seeds need four things to germinate and grow. They need water, light, the right temperature and oxygen. By its very nature, a seed is in a state of dormancy – your job is to unlock it. Give seeds soil that is wet and warm enough and off they will go. Warmth is perhaps more important than anything, if it's too cold for you to be outside it's probably too cold for the seeds. As the old saying goes, the soil isn't warm enough for sowing unless you can sit on it with your pants down.

There is a general rule of thumb that the bigger the seed, the deeper it needs to be to germinate. For instance, light is so essential for tiny poppy seeds that they won't germinate if they are buried; they have to sit on the surface of the soil. Beans, however, need to be covered with soil, otherwise a seedling will struggle to get its roots down deep enough and will fall over when it sprouts – seeds root first and shoot later. If your soil tends to be heavy and wet, it is worth sowing spring sowings a little nearer the surface than the standard recommended depth, as cold, wet soil will often rot dry seed.

If you look at a sprouted bean and see how small and delicate the roots are, then you'll understand why a seed likes soft, gentle soil to grow in. However, if you've ever walked across a farmer's fields, they are full of lumps, stones and things that gardening books tell you to get rid of at all cost. Farmers don't have time to go over their fields with a rake creating the finest tilth. The point is that a well-tilled seedbed is a good starting point and makes life easier, but if your soil refuses to break down into the perfect fine crumbly bed, don't give up. Just make sure you sow in the right conditions. Seeds are tough and designed to go it alone, they will come up pretty much whatever you sow them into.

Previous page:
Pricking out young seedlings by holding the seed leaves and supporting the roots. Opposite page: **Seeds come in all manner of shapes and sizes.** Left: **For something like lettuce, it's often easiest to scatter the seed liberally over the surface and then lightly cover with compost.**

Once your bed is ready for sowing, you need to water. Only water the area where you will sow seeds – this way you won't water the weed seeds as well.

How to sow

It's a bad idea to open a packet of seeds and pour from it straight into the soil. You have no control, seeds go everywhere and you'll waste more than you germinate. Instead pour a quantity of seed into the palm of your hand and, if the seeds are small, move them onto the top line, your heart line. With a little practice you will be able to open and close your hand so that the seeds move down your heart line as if they are on a conveyor belt. For larger seeds like radish or spinach, I like to take a little pinch from the palm of my hand

and carefully drop one seed after another. Being an adept seed sower is a matter of some pride – the more you practise, the better you get.

A good seed packet will tell you when, how and where to sow. It's important to sow at the right depth and to space seeds as it suggests or you could end up wasting a whole load. A point will arrive when you no longer need to check the packet; its information will be logged in your head along with telephone numbers and trivial pursuit facts, but until then keep checking.

Making choices

When you're starting a new garden, choose annuals and vegetables to get you going. Few perennials flower in their first year and the plants take time to bulk up from seed. Do have a go if you want to, but check the seed packet and know that it will be a while before you have bountiful plants. If you have a great desire for a plant or two of lavender in your garden, for example, it makes more sense to spend your money on a plant or take cuttings (more in Chapter Five), rather than starting from seed.

Vegetables

Choose vegetables with your stomach and purse in mind. Onions are cheap to buy and, to be honest, there's not a huge difference in taste, so it might not be worth growing them yourself. Lettuce leaves, on the other hand, particularly off-beat salad leaves such as spicy, colourful ones or cut-and-come-again varieties should be prized for home growing. A sun-warmed tomato straight off the vine, wrapped in a basil leaf, makes a mockery of any tomato you buy from a shop and everyone should have at least one summer when they savour this experience. If you're gardening in a small space then looks matter too, choose for colour and shape as well as taste so that plants really earn their space.

Seed companies are quick to recognise a trend and many now offer varieties that are particularly suited to growing in containers. Italian seed companies tend to be the most generous; maybe it's something to do with their love of food as their seed packets are full to the brim. But the back of the packet can often offer baffling diagrams of when to, or hilarious translations of how to sow.

If all you have is a windowsill, porch or neglected front garden, herbs are the way to go. Fresh herbs make such a difference to food; they can turn an emergency frozen meal into something tasty and make a home-made meal extraordinary. On the whole, they

Opposite page: **To sow in a row, create a line and then scatter seeds evenly down it. Next cover the line up and then water.**
Below: **Dahlias have long-lasting flowers that are superb in vases.**

are easy to grow. Most Mediterranean – herbs, basil, oregano, rosemary and whatnot – need sun for at least half the day. Mint, parsley, sorrel and chervil (flat leaf parsley) will grow in shade, but not deep shade.

Flowers

If you hanker after flowers, choose from hundreds of annuals, biennials and perennials. Whatever your whim, you can choose for scent, for colour or for picking. The only caveat is to beware of packets offering mixed colours. Unless they are all pastels, they too often turn out to be a garish version of the packet photo.

Seed typically stores for much longer than the sell-by date on the packet. The best way to store your seed is in your fridge. A half-used packet will work just as well next year, and probably for several years after that, if you tape up the flap and keep the packet in a container in the fridge. It is very important that the container is airtight as moisture quickly degrades seed.

Some large seed houses offer old stock at discount prices and this is one way of getting some really

interesting stuff at bargain prices (see my recommended companies on p.175). As the seed is past its first season, germination may be reduced, but rarely to the point where you don't get anything coming up, and an abundance of cheap seed will let you experiment and try new things.

The best seed is free, and there are loads of ways to get it. You may find it on a walk, get some from neighbours or seed-swapping events (see Chapter Eight), take it from fruit or save your own. You can also join various organisations that specialise in creating seed banks of heirloom or garden varieties. Usually for the price of the membership you get to choose from an amazing range of varieties.

Growing heirloom varieties

Heirloom vegetables and flowers are varieties that have been around for decades and are pollinated by bees and other insects rather than by humans. Naturally pollinated varieties are known as open-pollinated. Around the 1950s, horticulture began seriously developing increasing numbers of hybrid plants on a wide scale. Hybrid plants are artificially cross-pollinated. Many of these hybrids are F1 cultivars, which are bred for particular characteristics like higher yields and more uniform size – many would say that these characteristics are favoured over taste or smell. F1 stands for first filial generation. This means you select two parents with characteristics you like and produce first-year hybrid seed. Seed produced by the first year's generation won't reliably produce exact copies of that hybrid, and often loses its yield potential. What this means to the home gardener or farmer is that you can't save this seed for next year. If you want that cultivar again you have to buy it.

There is nothing wrong with F1 hybrids per se. F1 food crops have done a lot for farming and feeding people. But their introduction has meant less variety and choice, and for some farmers it has meant the loss of a way to support themselves. Everyone should grow at least one heirloom variety in his or her garden. Seeds saved from heirloom varieties will come true to type and will also adapt to your local conditions. When you save them you widen the gene pool for the next generation. When you harvest heirloom vegetables, you get to taste a little bit of history, and sometimes that taste is mind blowing.

Above: **Recycled seed trays. First, melt drainage holes through the plastic (top left). Fill with compost almost to the top and scatter seeds (top right). Gently firm seeds into the compost (bottom) and water (see overleaf).**

Where to sow seeds

Many seeds are happy sown direct into the ground, some are unhappy anywhere else, and some prefer alternative nursery accommodation.

Most vegetable seeds (except Mediterranean types) and hardy annuals have a sporting chance if you sow them directly into the ground, but you're more in control if you sow some varieties into compost and transplant seedlings into the soil. This particularly applies to any that need specific conditions in terms of temperature, light and water.

Another reason to avoid direct sowing is that you're not the only one interested in your seeds and seedlings. Slugs, snails, mice and birds are also on the look out, and it's easier to defend your bounty before

it's planted out. If you can get seedlings to a decent size, they stand a better chance of surviving attacks, and if the worst happens and nearly everything you plant out is munched to death, you can have reserves left in a tray to fill the gaps.

Allotment gardeners or those of you who garden in a community patch should start your seedlings at home where you can keep an eye on them every day. If you can only visit your plot at weekends in spring, this will save a lot of heartache over munched or frozen seedlings.

If you are not going to sow straight into soil, you will need good compost. Multi-purpose compost does not make the best seed compost; it's best to make your own or at least amend the multi-purpose. The best seed compost is a mix of one third multi-purpose or homemade compost, one third leaf mould and one third vermiculite. Leaf mould is wonderful stuff for seedlings and a lovely home-made luxury. Don't worry if you don't have any, you can get away with vermiculite and compost.

If you don't yet have any home-made compost either, buy ready-made seed compost. Always read the ingredients list: many companies put non-organic fertilisers or peat in their mix – the first are unnecessary, the second is unsustainable.

Either sow into seed trays (you can buy half sizes which are useful for small gardens) or modules. I like modules for vegetables as you can put two or three little seeds in each module, thinning out the weaker ones and letting the strongest grow to plug size. Plugs are easy to transplant, and you can pop a plug straight into a gap when you harvest something else, so you don't waste a spot of space.

It's tempting to sow a whole tray with one packet, but hold back. Say you have thirty modules, that's potentially thirty identical tomato plants that you're either going to have to pot on or throw away. Instead, work out how many plants you want and then throw in a few extra as back-up. Either sow a selection of varieties in separate rows, or fill the tray with other plants with similar germination requirements.

What to sow where

Sow direct into the ground
Carrots, beetroot, radish, salsify, red orache (*Atriplex hortensis* var. *rubra*)

Cornflowers (*Centaurea cyanus*), marigolds (*Calendula officinalis*/ top left), scarlet pimpernel (*Linum grandiflorum*), love-in-the-mist (*Nigella damscena*), honesty (*Lunaria annua*), annual poppies (*Papaver commutatum*), (*Papaver rhoeas*), (*Papaver somniferum*), godetias, nasturtiums

Sow either in pots, trays or direct
Lettuce, oriental greens, brassicas, spinach, peas, beans, Swiss chard (top right), land cress, parsley, coriander

Sweet peas (*Lathyrus odoratus*, best in pots), California poppies (*Eschscholzia californica*), (*Cerinthe major* var. *purpurascens*), stocks (*Matthiola longipetala* subsp. *bicornis*), pansies but (*Viola* x *wittrockiana*) in pots

Sow only in trays, modules or pots
Courgettes, cucumbers, melons, tomatoes, peppers, aubergines, onions, chillies, basil

Cosmos (*Cosmos bipinnatus*), morning glory (*Ipomea*), mint, dahlias, busy Lizzies (*Impatiens*)

Left: **A recycled bottle waterer.** Opposite page: **How to prick out.**
Carefully tease the seedlings apart, making sure not to tear the roots,
and pot on into individual pots.

Watering seedlings

Seedlings need gentle watering. Great gushes of water from a watering can will disturb the soil and roots and knock the seedlings over. Either use a watering can with a fine rose, or use an old bottle, preferably with a wide mouth. Poke small holes concentrically around the lid of the bottle and fill it with water. Keep it on the windowsill with the trays, then it will be sun-warmed when you come to use it and your seedlings will love you for it. Seed compost should be kept moist. If you put your finger on the surface, it should feel damp, but not wet. If you have covered your seeds with a polythene bag or clear lid, it should mist up with condensation.

Pricking out

Seedlings, especially those grown in small trays, quickly outgrow their space. At this point you need to prick them out. This is when you give each individual seedling its own space. You'll often find you have more seedlings than space. Be ruthless at this stage or your home will get overrun with plants that are too tender to go outside. When space is an issue, prick out 50 per cent more than you think you need, which is a generous allowance for failure, and no more.

Never handle a seedling by its stem; it is so young and tender that you'll do it damage. The same goes for the roots; instead hold a seedling by its leaves. Depending on its stage of growth, your seedling may have two different types of leaves: baby ones, called seed leaves, and true leaves. Seed leaves feed the plant until the true leaves appear – this is why seed compost doesn't need food. Always hold the seed leaves, as these are tougher. You can use a pencil, chopstick or pointed plant label to separate seedlings – support the weight of the roots with the pencil as you lift each seedling from its compost.

The next stage is potting on. Seeds started in trays will be hungry by the time they've outgrown their space. It's usual to plant them into a 7.5cm pot so they can start to develop a proper root system. I sow most vegetables directly into the larger modular seed trays and let them stay there till planting out. Peas and beans are best sown straight into 7.5cm pots or yogurt pots.

Potting on at seedling stage is simple. Fill your pots or modules with compost, make a holes in the centre with a pencil and drop the seedling in. Seedling roots are damaged by firming the compost around them – gently push the compost with the end of the pencil and follow with a gentle water to firm them in.

Solving problems

If your seedlings are long and floppy, it means that they have had too much heat and not enough light. Rescue them from getting leggy by burying them almost up to the seed leaves when potting on. This should work fine as long as you don't overwater.

Light is vital at seedling stage and some gardeners put their trays under light boxes to make sure seedlings get enough light. I don't personally think this is a good plan, for seedlings or the environment. The most likely cause of leggy seedlings is that you started your seeds too soon and nature can't catch up. It is surprising how well seedlings are adapted to the seasons; a week or so may make little impact on us, but seedlings can utilise every second of extra light.

Damping off

Sometimes all your seedlings seem to be doing well, then the centre ones die and, as soon as you turn your back, the rest join them. This is called damping off. It's a broad term to describe a group of fungi that kill seedlings. Usually the stem rots at the base, which is why it falls over, sometimes the leaves change colour first.

There is no cure for damping off. If it happens, cut your losses and bin the lot before it spreads to other seedlings. Prevention is the only solution. The fungi are spread in water and soil, so don't overwater – the usual sign of overwatering is a green tinge on the surface of your compost. It can be a good idea to cover your seedlings with vermiculite instead of soil – vermiculite holds available water until the seedlings need it.

One solution, if you are getting a lot of damping off, is to microwave your soil. Seven minutes in a microwave-safe dish will thoroughly sterilise your soil.

Just don't cook anything immediately afterwards as the microwave smells a bit funny for a while.

You must also keep everything scrupulously clean. Wash your containers thoroughly in hot water and biodegradable household disinfectant before using them. And make sure there is good ventilation around your seedlings; open the window a little on sunny days.

Poor germination

If your seeds don't germinate, it will be for one of three reasons. Perhaps you buried them too deep, which usually goes along with overwatering. If you dig around, you'll find them rotting. If the conditions are right – correct temperature, light and good compost – you don't need to water your seed trays until the first seedling leaves appear.

Temperature is another factor. Seeds will stay locked in dormancy until the right temperature. Your seed packet will tell you the ideal temperature for germination, so if you have persistent problems get a soil thermometer. I became a much, much better gardener once I knew the temperature of my soil.

The third possibility is that you are just being impatient. Some seeds take less than a week to start life but others, such as trees, can take over a year.

A propagator does hugely increase the speed and the range of what you grow. If you get hooked on seed sowing, it's a worthwhile investment. There are long, thin versions designed to go on a windowsill, which are useful for small apartments. If you've got more space, a covered front porch or an old greenhouse, how about starting a sow-op with your friends. You'll germinate everything, your friends will provide the space to grow and you can pool the produce.

Left: These coriander seeds have grown leggy from too much heat and too little light. However, they are still good to eat as microveg.

Cold frames are a half-way house between cosseted indoor life and the big bad world.

Hardening off

Seedlings may be perfectly happy indoors, but life can't stay that way and they will have to venture into the great outdoors – what a shock that can be. The trick to getting your seedlings from indoors to out is called hardening off. One of the most effective methods is using a cold frame. This keeps the worst of frost, wind and rain off the seedlings and allows them time to acclimatise.

A cold frame is basically a box with a clear lid, and easy to make. You could make do with a thick cardboard box with a sheet of plastic or glass over the top – the polystyrene boxes that fishmongers use are great – or you can build an instant version using bricks and an old windowpane.

For a more permanent solution, you can build a decent-sized cold frame from reclaimed pallet wood. For the roof, you can buy perspex or glass or, if you're lucky, you might find a window and frame intact in a skip. These make the best lids as you can open the window in increments to acclimatise the seedlings.

Seedlings need to spend around two weeks in a cold frame before they are hardy. Open the lid during the day and close it at night. On bright days, they will need shade – plastic netting or old net curtains over the top of the box does a good job.

Building a cold frame from old pallets

Materials

2 pallets
150cm of 40mm x 15mm round
    sawn timber for battens
Sheet of Perspex
40mm oval wire nails
Wood saw
Clawhammer/ spade
Gloves

To create the boxes

Try to hunt for the strongest pallets, all of a similar size. Never take returnable pallets, but look for ones marked 'Non-returnable'. With your spade, carefully prise the pallets apart, removing the nails as you go. You will need 20–24 lengths of pallet timber. This is easy to write and often very hard to do. Prising something that never wanted to come apart requires patience. Look for new pallets where possible: wet, rotting or old timber just cracks immediately.

Make the back panel by nailing six lengths of timber together, with a length of batten at each end.

Make the front panel by nailing four lengths of timber together, with a length of batten at each end

You can either make the sides out of more pallet timber or perspex and battens.

Make the side panel by nailing six lengths of timber together, with a length of pallet timber at each end.

Mark the height of the front panel on one end of each of the side panels.

Use the wood saw to cut the top slope into each side panel, then nail the side panels on to the front and back panels.

The perspex lid can be weighed down with some bricks or, if you are feeling handy, you could create a frame and attach it to the box with hinges.

Late sowing

I love seed sowing, but I also know how easy it is to miss the moment to sow – and there's your tomatoes gone for another year. Or not. Luckily, you can often cheat.

Should you miss the right weather for sowing Mediterranean herbs, such as basil, don't worry, the supermarket has done it for you. If you look closely, you'll see that those pots of basil, parsley and coriander are just loads of leggy seedlings. growing together. You can carefully tease them apart and you've instantly got lots of basil plants. Trim the roots and pinch out the top sets of leaves, then plant them in containers or in the ground. Give them a good soak and some liquid fertiliser, such as nettle or comfrey tea (see p. 113) or seaweed, and they'll soon be happy.

If you really don't have time to sow or you seem to have hit a rut of bad batches, bypass the whole stage and get mail-order plugs online or from catalogues. They're not cheap, but all you have to do is plant them and they're away. It may not be the thriftiest way to garden, but don't beat yourself up about how you get started – growing from plugs is not inferior to growing from seed, just more expensive.

On the other hand, plugs of bedding plants can be incredibly cheap, and since many bedding plants need heat to germinate, buying them is often the best solution, especially if you've got limited germinating space. They're rather an old-fashioned thing to sell, and you're more likely to pick them up from traditional nurseries and ironmongers rather than DIY sheds.

Above: **Good to go. Plugs are an easy way to start growing vegetables.** Opposite page: **Thinning beetroot seedlings. Baby beet leaves are delicious, so don't waste thinnings.**

When to plant out

All tender plants, including all seedlings, have to be planted out after the last frost. But if you find yourself with rows of little plants and a freak weather report, just get some fleece, newspaper or even branches and cover your plants overnight. A healthy plant is surprisingly strong and will make it through. If you're worried about the weather, most internet weather sites have worked out that they've got a gardening audience and offer alerts on frosts and even advice on when to plant out. Google 'garden weather' and you're bound to find a site to suit.

Thinning

Plants need space, so thinning is vital. Imagine if you asked a bunch of schoolkids to stand shoulder to shoulder, then asked them to raise their arms up slowly, as if for a star jump. You'd get lots of little kids bashing each other's ears. But if you removed every other kid from the line, they'd have more space and, if you thinned them out to one in three, they'd be in star-jumping heaven. That's the principle of thinning. It may seem an extravagant waste to take tiny little seedlings and throw them away – you can nibble vegetable thinnings as you go – but if you don't do it, none of them will grow properly. The back of the packet of seed will say what distance to thin to, but if you don't have that to hand, then guesstimate by imagining what size the vegetable will be when you want to eat it, then add another 10cm or so either side and you'll not be far off. The more space you give, the larger the vegetable, particularly with root veg like carrots and parsnips.

In general, the best time to thin a crop is as soon as the seedlings are large enough to handle. The trick is not to thin all at once. So if it says to thin to 30cm, thin to 5cm one week, 10cm the next, and so on. If you immediately thin to your final spacing, chances are that a slug will come along for lunch and you'll find you have a row of three plants, instead of ten. You can eat almost all vegetable thinnings, apart from radishes. If you are harvesting your thinnings for supper then use scissors, snipping off the young leaves at soil level. The roots will die back and you won't have to spend hours cleaning soil from tiny seedlings.

Planting out

Planting out is joyously simple. You need something to dig with (which can be anything from a soup spoon to a spade), something helpful to put at the bottom of the hole, and something to water with. The helpful thing at the bottom depends on your plants. Drought-loving plants such as cacti, succulents and lavenders hate wet feet so they'd appreciate grit to help with drainage. Roses and clematis would be pleased with moisture-rich food such as semi-rotted compost, and seedlings would like worm casts. Well-rotted organic matter – compost – is an important addition to any perennial planting hole. This will act as a source of food for the roots and will improve the soil conditions. You should consider spending as much on the hole as the plant. This doesn't just mean money, it means time spent getting the conditions right – good drainage, food and moisture.

Water is the most essential factor. Forget that and you'll be marching your plant off to heaven. If the weather has been dry and your soil is thin, water the hole before you plant. Fill it right to the top and then walk away and do another job. After ten minutes or so, it will have drained away and the hole will be in perfect condition for you to plant into.

Any plant that has sat too long in a container has roots bound together, usually in a spiral shape from a round container. These need to be teased apart, otherwise the roots will continue to swirl around, never breaking out into the real world and, after a year or so, you may find the plant dead. If you pull it up, the rootball will be perfectly in the shape of the container in which it arrived as the roots will never have ventured out into the soil. This happens because the soil the plant was grown in was soft and easy and the soil in your garden was not. You have to be brutal to be kind. I tease out the roots by taking my pruners and hacking liberally into the rootball – if it's a little plug, I'm kinder and just chop off the bottom centimetre instead. Wherever you cut, the plant will go into emergency action and produce new root hairs, and one root will branch into two and so on.

Do make sure you plant deep enough. Too often it's rather hard work to make a deep hole, so a plant gets jammed in with some of the roots exposed to the air. These will die off. It is safer to bury most flowering plants 5cm or so deeper than the level of soil they came in. This will form a bushier, sturdier plant. For seedlings, make sure that the bottom leaves don't sit on the soil surface or they will rot in wet weather.

Where there is a rule, there's always an exception. Never bury a tree or shrub deeper than its nursery line (the level where it's growing in the pot). Trees and woody shrubs hate having their bark buried, it begins to rot and slowly this kills the plant. For this reason, also make sure that the base isn't covered with mulch.

Planting a tree or large shrub

A tree hole needs to be much bigger than the pot the tree came in. The best holes are square because the roots hit a corner then are forced off in another direction. Round holes and round pots can mean spiralling roots, so the tree falls over in the first big storm. The bottom of the hole should have good drainage, so you may need to add grit on heavy soil. You shouldn't put manure or rich compost in, for two reasons. The roots like this too much and won't head off exploring and, if the soil is clay the manure rots, creating anaerobic conditions that kill the roots. You can add slow-release fertiliser, such as chicken pellets. I prefer to add something called mycorrhizal fungi. This is still a fairly newly available product, so I source it online; it's not a cheap product, but I find it the best.

Left: A good design trick is to mimic nature. Here foxgloves (*Digitalis viridiflora*) are placed before planting to create a drift, as they might be found in nature.

Mycorrhizal fungi grow into the tree roots and produce enzymes that make phosphorus and other nutrients available to the tree. This happens because the roots that become infected with the fungi, which form a fine network of thread-like strands, called hyphae. These extend the network of the roots. Out of a single root there may emerge up to three metres of hyphae. This allows the tree to explore more soil. I think this is really important, as instead of giving a concentration of food just around the rootball, you encourage the tree to explore the soil around, getting a more extensive rooting system and fending for itself. Slow-release fertilisers run out eventually, but it's hard to gauge when this is, and even harder for you to know how the roots are doing. Mycorrhizal fungi make for a more independent tree.

You should water the hole until it is filled to the brim at least once before planting and again once the tree is settled. A tree will need watering regularly for the first year of its new life in the ground, and that means every other week through the summer. Finally, you need a tree stake.

If all this seems too much fuss, sow acorns, chestnuts or cobnuts straight into the ground or plant free seedlings and let nature do the rest, with no staking and no watering – free trees tough it out on their own.

Staking

Staking is very important for newly established plants; tall, floppy plants such as delphiniums and climbers need something to grow up. A young root system isn't tough enough to support a plant in a strong wind. However, all plants need to rock around a little – a gentle rocking motion stimulates the roots and encourages them to anchor firmly. This is the reason that seedlings grow stronger if you gently run your hands over them to stroke them.

Most garden centres sell tree stakes fairly cheaply, or buy 50 x 50mm rough sawn timber and cut to length. A stake for a tree needs to be one third the length of the tree height. This allows the tree to flex in the wind, causing the trunk to increase in thickness and strength. The stake should be angled at 45 degrees into the ground.

Make sure that the tie between stake and plant can expand – either use a flexible material or loosen the tie as the tree grows. A cheap material for young trees and shrubs is an old pair of tights. 'Tight around the stake, loose around the plant' is the mantra for staking perennials, tomatoes and climbers. It is usual to make a figure-of-eight loop between the plant and stake,

Opposite page: **A shrub or tree needs to be planted into a hole just deep enough to take the rootball – never bury the stem. Gently tease out the roots into surrounding soil. Back fill, firm in and water.** Right: **Make sure the tie is tight around the stake and loose around the stem.**

doubling the tie around the stake. This will allow the plants just enough 'give' to move and grow without causing the tie to rub.

Bamboo canes are obvious garden stakes, but there are many other locally available materials. Dogwood (*Cornus*), willow (*Salix*) and hazel (*Corylus*) are prime candidates. Harvest poles during the winter and store somewhere dry for the summer. Willow roots easily as soon as it hits the ground; prevent this by covering the end with masking tape. Rolled steel bar often turns up in skips: 6-8mm diameter bars are very easy to bend into loops for climbers. If you can't easily bend it, place the steel around a lamppost or tree, roughly at the middle point of the length and then pull the two ends to your chest. It should bend into a U. It quickly rusts into an innocuous shade of brown.

Watering

Water is crucially important to a plant. Most of us know to water in a plant once we've planted it, but too many of us think we can let nature do the rest. There are good reasons why this doesn't work. Most plants are grown in a nursery where they might be watered every day, and they are definitely watered every week. Next they go to a garden centre where they're watered daily, and then they come home with you. Suddenly they go from a drink a day to cold turkey because you've put them in the ground, given them one last drink and expected the rain to do the rest. These plants need your help to adjust; they need you to give them a good drink at least once a week through the hot months. That way you'll still be looking at them the following year.

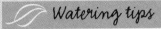
Watering tips

1. Every time you plant something, water it in well.

2. Plants in pots rely on you for water. In hot conditions, most plants need to be watered daily.

3. If you are planting in very dry ground, dig the hole, fill it with water and walk away. Come back, fill it with water again. Only then should you plant and you still need to water afterwards.

4. Make a moated island of soil around newly established plants, so when you water it won't all run off but will go straight to the roots.

5. Water pots and containers so that water appears right to the top of the container. Only then do you know that you have watered right the way through the pot.

6. Turkey basters are useful for removing excess water from the saucers of houseplants.

7. Plants love sun-warmed water. Leave a full bucket next to containers and young vegetables.

8. If you have space and a drainpipe that you can convert, get a waterbutt. You don't have to invest in a tailor-made one, but hunt in yard sales, online and in skips for industrial food barrels, old water-storage units and cider or beer barrels. Make sure that you know what the contents were and clean the tub out thoroughly before collecting water. Taps and convertors can be bought online or from shops selling beer-making kits.

9. Uncovered waterbutts will get mosquito larvae. Pour a small cup of vegetable oil into the water. It won't harm the plants, but will suffocate the larvae. Or you can add small goldfish, but take care not to drain all the water at once. Goldfish are resilient enough to need feeding only through the colder months.

10. If you're going away for the weekend, let your houseplants water themselves. Cut a few holes in the lid of a plastic water bottle, cut the bottom off, fill the bottle with water and insert it upside down into the compost. The water will slowly drip into the pots.

Opposite page:
Free water – by collecting rain you save money and the environment. Make sure you install your waterbutt in early spring, so you've saved enough water by summer.

Feeding your plants

All plants need certain elements to grow. Carbon, oxygen and hydrogen are the most important as these make up the chain for photosynthesis. Probably only first-year horticultural students can gleefully list every element that is needed, and why. The rest of us just need to know three – NPK. These stand for Nitrogen, Phosphorus and Potassium. They are most important because they are needed in larger quantities than other elements, and they need to be readily available to the plant. Most shop-bought general fertilisers are made up of various ratios of NPK.

Healthy soil naturally contains all these elements and many more. But poor, compacted soil may be lacking some of them, or they may be locked up in some other form and literally unavailable. I think I might go to my grave banging on about compost, but the message can't be underestimated. The best thing for your soil is your own compost. Absolutely no question. Organic matter – your compost – is manna to your soil. It provides an excellent source of nitrogen, it increases soil microbial activity, which means pathogens are kept down, and it increases worm activity which in turn opens up the soil and adds more air. And where there's air and moisture, there are nutrients.

If your soil is tired or your plants look hungry, give them compost first. The rule of thumb is a bucket of home-made compost per square metre of soil. It's just as important to add compost to pots: feed them with a layer on top. However, there is a point when you'll need other fertilisers, either because your compost isn't ready or when you are growing in containers. In the summer you will have to liquid-feed plants in pots or heavy croppers, such as tomatoes, every two weeks to promote good growth.

Seaweed is another good fertiliser for organic gardeners. This is a good source of organic matter, it's

Food science

N Nitrogen promotes leafy green growth. Too much delays flowers and fruiting; too little reduces yield and causes leaves to go yellow.

P Phosphorus is essential for flower and fruit formation. Too little and you get purple stems and leaves, stunted growth and poor yields of fruit and flowers. Phosphorus must be applied near the roots for a plant to take it up.

K Potassium is necessary for cell division in the roots. It also increases drought tolerance and hardiness, and enhances both flavour and colour of fruit and vegetable crops. Too little results in low yields, mottled, spotted or curled leaves or a scorched or burnt look to the leaves.

high in nitrogen and contains numerous other elements. If you can get hold of fresh seaweed, then compost it or dry it out a bit and use it as mulch. Any type is good, but remember to harvest only stuff that has washed up on the beach. This has been ripped up from the sea bed and is now going to die. Never harvest growing seaweed, as many varieties are now considered endangered. If you can't gather it yourself, you can buy liquid seaweed that you dilute and water onto plants. Seaweed is a tonic for stimulating good, healthy growth and best used as a supplement, rather like taking extra vitamins when you've got a cold.

Chicken pellets are a good source of slow-release fertiliser, particularly valuable for pots. It's a good idea to add these to your containers at the beginning of the season. They are concentrated and no substitute for bulky organic matter, so you should use compost if you're trying to improve your soil.

Comfrey or nettle tea

Some plants are so packed with energy and nutrients that they can be successfully used to feed others. Even if you have to buy comfrey plants to start with, once they are established you may never need to buy commercially made plant food. Nettles are not quite so powerful, but always free.

Comfrey is a deep-rooted, hardy perennial that is found throughout Europe. Its leaves are high in potash, a source of potassium important for cell division, and also have good levels of nitrogen and phosphate. Three forms of comfrey make good all-round fertilisers.

Common wild forms, *Symphytum officinale* and *Symphytum asperum*, are useful as leaves for compost or for tea. 'Bocking 14' is a cultivar of Russian comfrey (*Symphytum* x *uplandicum*). Specially developed as an organic fertiliser, this form doesn't flower and instead puts all its energy into producing leaves that make an excellent brew. Comfrey can also be put on the compost to act as an activator and speed up the

Below: **Collecting comfrey. If you find a source growing naturally, make sure you ask the landowner before harvesting and don't strip the plant bare.**

composting process. I tend to grow a clump next to my compost for this reason.

Symphytum officinale and *S. asperum* both seed freely. If you know someone with a plant, ask them for a division or for some seed to sow in autumn. 'Bocking 14' is sterile, so you have to take root cuttings.

Comfrey tea

Made from steeped leaves, this can be used as a general-purpose fertiliser or pick-me-up. On newly established plants, harvest only half the leaves and send any flowering stalks to the compost bin. Otherwise harvest by cutting the leaves right down to the ground. Established plants can be harvested up to four times a year. Stuff as many fresh or wilted leaves as possible into a container with a tightly fitting lid and fill it with water. Exact quantities aren't too important. Weigh the lid down with bricks and after ten or so days your brew will start to ferment.

You'll know it's doing well when you can barely get near the container, as comfrey stinks when it's rotting. That's where the tight-fitting lid comes in. I almost relish the smell now because I know that what most offends my nose will please the plants. My comfrey making is not an exact art and I don't tend to dilute it, but some methods make a concentrated solution which stores well. As a rule, I never use comfrey on houseplants because it just smells too much indoors.

Nettles also make an effective tea. Young, spring nettles make the strongest concoction. Like comfrey, when it really starts to smell you'll know it's ready.

Right: Chop up lots and lots of leaves and add water. By excluding light you speed up the decomposition process, but wait at least two weeks to brew. Filter the brew and water onto plants every fortnight through the growing season.

Pruning
& propagating

The truth is that only practice, time and a good manual will make you a good pruner. You are not born good at this job, you get there through trial and error. It's the same with propagating, which just means ways of producing more plants. Once you've learned the basics, you can turn the one plant you could afford at the garden centre into seven, you can take cuttings of things you like from friends' gardens, and before you know it you'll have a garden full of wonderful things.

The rough guide to pruning

Firstly, you need to understand why you prune. It's done for three reasons – to remove unhealthy material, to control the size and shape of a plant, and to increase flowering and fruiting. First you remove the three 'd's – dead, dying or diseased material. Then you take out any branches that are crossing because these can rub against each other, leading to weak spots that provide potential opportunities for diseases and pests to get in.

Most pruning has to be done because a plant has outgrown its space. Take it slowly, savour each moment, consider the plant at all times. Pruning is the epitome of slow gardening. It is all too easy to get carried away and chop out far more than is necessary, but that usually means several years of puny growth. If an adrenaline rush of slash and burn steps in and you're verging dangerously near hacking the thing to within a centimetre of its life, then move away from the plant and go have a cup of tea.

It's generally a bad idea to prune in spring after new shoots appear because this weakens the plant and influences how it will produce more growth. Early autumn is another bad time as many plants will try to respond with a new flush of growth, which will then get hit by the frost. For example, olive trees pruned in late summer or early autumn will gamely send out new shoots, but this tender growth won't have time to harden off before winter and will definitely get blasted in the frost.

There are as many ways to prune as there are plants. There's no point in trying to summarise pruning down to a few steps. And you don't need to know it all. You do not need to know how to prune apple trees if all you have is a buddleja. Find out what you do have in your garden and go research. But if you are keen to have a go without a manual, first get to grips with a bit of basic botany.

Left: **Fast-growing shrubs such as buddleja can be cut back hard each year. This way, you can control shape and size.**

Trees

All trees and shrubs produce buds. The topmost bud is called the apical bud and has what is known as apical dominance. This means that it produces hormones that restrict the growth of buds further down. This stops overcrowding and competition. Look at a tree: you'll see the very topmost stem has apical dominance and is leading the way vertically. If you remove its tip or bud you will divert the source of hormones to the lower set of buds, allowing them to develop into stems. In turn, they restrict the buds below them.

This is the principle behind pinching out young seedlings to get bushy growth. You remove the tip so that the buds below can develop. But if you do this to a tree you may unintentionally affect the overall height of the tree. This is particularly true of conifers and upright-shaped trees with an obvious leader. If you cut it out you basically ruin the tree.

Tree-pruning tips

If you need to take out a big limb where you'll need a big ladder, save yourself potential serious injury and get in a tree surgeon.

Only tackle small limbs that you can easily reach and where you don't need a chain saw.

Never try and cut off a whole branch in one go; even smallish branches are surprisingly heavy and hard to control with only one hand. Cut in sections to lesson the weight.

Cut underneath the branch first, this partial cut stops the bark from tearing down the trunk if the branch accidentally breaks.

Always try to prune deciduous trees when they are not in leaf.

Shrubs

With shrubs, removing the top bud is rarely disastrous, in fact it often leads to the kind of bushy growth that is desirable. But where you cut does matter. If you have a branch that needs to be removed because it's in the way, don't chop it in half – this will get it out the way for now, but it will quickly produce side stems, which in turn will grow back right in the way again. Instead remove the stem right down at the base of the shrub, ideally in early spring. Always prune dogwoods (*Cornus*), willows (*Salix*) and hazel (*Corylus*) this way. It's also the best way of pruning for foliage effects. *Catalpa bignonioides*, eucalyptus, the smoke bush *Cotinus coggygria* 'Royal Purple', limes (*Tilia cordata*) and the foxglove tree (*Paulownia tomentosa*) all respond well if you cut stems back to within two or three buds at the base, or to a framework such as a pollard.

Most prunings can head straight for the compost, but some can have a second life. Colourful dogwoods, hazels and willows are easy to bend and can be made into simple low fences or supports for climbing plants such as sweet peas (*Lathyrus odoratus*) and beans. If you've got lots of prunings, you could get into making all sorts of fun garden structures from bentwood.

Perennials

Perennials are plants that spend the winter dormant, sending their energy back into rootballs underground, emerging again in spring. By late winter, it's time to cut them back, although if you want to be wildlife-friendly save some till spring as lots of helpful insects sleep in dead plant stems. Cut woody stems down to the ground to allow for new growth; if some has already appeared, take care not to cut off any new shoots. A perennial is ready to cut back when it has virtually no green growth and only old brown stems and flowers.

Left: Prunings don't have to be composted, they can be used to make fences or plant supports. I've used willow and dogwood here. If you can't use the material immediately, then keep it in a bucket of water so the wood remains flexible.

Above: Cut shrubs such as hazel, dogwood, buddleja and willow right back to one or two buds. Top right: A good cut should have a slant so that rain-water runs off. Right: A bad cut – this cut was too far from the bud and has left an unsightly dead bit. Far right: Prune out any damaged material.

Pruning can also help many perennials into a second flowering half-way through the season. A good indicator that a perennial is gearing up for a second flush is when you have leggy, tatty, tall growth and lots of fresh new growth at the bottom. When you see this, prune off all the old growth and this will promote even more new shoots.

Left and below: Ornamental grass can be given an annual trim. If it goes brown in autumn, then trim. If it is green in autumn, wait till early spring.

Bamboos

Bamboos that have overstayed their welcome can be brought back into control with a late summer or early spring clean. Let air and light into overcrowded clumps by removing all old canes at the base, leaving only healthy young canes. Keep the prunings if they're straight to use as home-grown stakes. You can really get stuck in, it's hard to kill a bamboo – even if you chop off every cane the plant will still spring back to life. If a bamboo has really outgrown its space, arm yourself with loppers, saws and a good spade. Eat a couple of chocolate bars as it's hefty work. Then start hacking the rootball into sections, each with a healthy stem or two. Replant one of these and give the rest away to friends, but make sure that they have plenty of space or they might not thank you in years to come – if bamboos like you they can try to take over your garden.

Grasses

Most ornamental grasses need an annual trim. If it turns brown by late summer, trim it back to the ground in winter. If it's still green in autumn, trim it back to the ground in early spring. Evergreen grasses just need a good hairbrush, take a spring rake and brush the clump vigorously and old stuff will quickly fall out. Do not cut evergreen grasses back to the ground – they don't like it.

Right: Deadheading prolongs flowering, but if you want to save seed ease off towards the end of the season or else you won't have any to harvest. Opposite page, top: Pinching out encourages bushy growth. Bottom: Deadheading violas. Pinching out with your thumb and forefinger is easiest on smaller plants.

Pinching out

This creates bushy growth, which is why you're advised to pinch out so many types of seedlings – instead of a tall spindly plant you'll get a compact bushy one. Coleus also needs pinching out. Pinch out vigorous leaders to produce strong healthy side shoots – nip out the top when a young plant has reached five or six leaf joints.

Deadheading

Deadheading helps some plants to produce more flowers. The more you deadhead, the more flowers you get. However, if you want to collect seed, you have to stop deadheading in time to allow the plant to set seed. This is also the reason why deadheading causes more flowers – the plant is desperately trying to produce progeny. If you remove the flower and don't let it go to seed, it will try time and time again.

Annuals generally don't respond well to deadheading. With certain bedding plants, such as petunias and pansies, deadheading is traditionally considered to prolong the flowering season, but as a student I was made to do a trial on deadheading versus doing nothing. There was very little in it. I think the long and short of it is, if you like deadheading, go forth and deadhead and, if you can't be bothered, don't worry about it.

On the other hand, many perennials and most roses do well under a strict regime. You can literally just cut off dead flowers or stems on most plants, but with roses it's best to cut back to a healthy bud. This new bud will produce new shoots and, with luck, you'll get a second and even a third re-bloom. Some roses including *Rosa rugosa* are grown for their spectacular hips as much as their flowers. If you cut off the flowers you won't get hips, so stop deadheading these by late June to give the hips time to form.

Pruning to manipulate plants

Many perennial plants can be manipulated for your benefit by pruning. You can extend or renew blooming, encourage new lush growth, reduce plant height, keep plants in their own spaces, and prevent or control pests and diseases.

Cutting back for height control

Pruning to remove foliage is known as cutting back. If you're on a windy, exposed site, whether it's a roof garden or hill, you'll need to spend a good amount of your spring and summer staking. One way to reduce this is to cut back summer- and autumn-flowering perennials in early to mid June before they flower, to keep their overall height down. In most cases this will cause more, but smaller, flowers. I don't think this is very noticeable and is a fine payoff for less staking.

This form of pruning is still experimental; there's a lot of research to be done and all plants respond differently due to climate conditions, age and vigour. But in general this method delays blooming by at least two weeks, and the closer you cut the plant to its normal flowering date, the greater the delay in flowering. If you always go away for part of the summer, you can use this technique to make sure you come back to some flowers. It's worth trying on a few tough summer perennials. Balloon flowers (*Platycodon grandiflorus*) tend to flop, but if you prune them back to half their height in June you'll not need to stake. *Phlox maculata* and *Phlox paniculata* can be treated similarly. Cut back by one half when the plant is just coming into bud and you'll end up with a more compact plant.

Many autumn-flowering perennials make likely candidates. In wet summers, *Sedum* 'Autumn Joy' and other cultivars usually grow too lush and then flop to show an unsightly woody centre. Chopping their foliage back at bud stage by one half or two thirds will delay flowering, but you won't need to stake. Rudbeckias often grow way too tall on lush soils and then flop and fold in the slightest wind. Solve this by chopping off two thirds of growth just as buds appear, usually around early to mid June. Joe Pye weed, (*Eupatorium maculatum*) will grow to a hefty 4.5m in a good summer. This is great if you have the space, otherwise chop by at least half in June for a more manageable plant – you can go as low as 30cm, but the plant will not flower below 1m.

Asters often flop to expose their less attractive middles after a wet summer, which completely spoils their lovely autumn blooms. I've taken to chopping them by one half, sometimes even more for a very tall variety, in late May to get an improved habit. In England I find it doesn't affect the flowering time.

Doing the Chelsea chop

If experimental cutting back is not for you, this method is much loved, tried and tested. Traditionally growers would chop back their spring- and early summer-flowering perennials just after the famous Chelsea Flower Show in London. Hence the name. This would cause any unsold plants to grow a fine flush of new growth in time for later summer sales. The trick with the Chelsea chop is to be utterly brutal and cut the whole plant back to its base. After your brutality, give the plant lots of love with some food and lots of water – the results are amazing.

Good Chelsea candidates

Many hardy geraniums flower in May and June. Once they've finished flowering they tend to become leggy and unsightly. Cut them hard back right to their bases and they'll respond with new lush growth and a second flowering in good seasons. With some varieties

the old flowering stems fall outside the clump and a new flush of leaves appears in the middle; with these just trim off the old stuff.

The only hardy geraniums I don't prune back this way are 'Roxanne' which has lovely blue flowers in late summer and 'Ann Folkard'. This is one of the first to start blooming and doesn't quit till the first frost if left alone. Its sprawling habit makes it useful for hiding the bases of roses and clematis.

Brunnera macrophylla is spring flowering, with lovely delicate forget-me-not flowers. It can be sheared right the way to its base once it finishes flowering, to give new foliage and flowers. Pulmonarias also flower in spring and often have unsightly foliage by summer. After they've flowered in spring, cut back all the old foliage, you'll often find new leaves coming up through the centres. Water the plants well and they'll respond with sporadic flowering in a mild summer.

Once delphiniums finish flowering, be brave and chop the plants right back to the ground – the whole thing. You need to be quick here and not let them start setting seed. Feed and water every week (this is very important as you're asking a lot of the plant) and you'll get a whole second flush of blooms in late summer. You will need to keep slugs off the young foliage, and if you cut back hard every year you do tend to exhaust the plants, but you'll get great displays while they last.

Oriental poppies (*Papaver orientale*) don't produce lovely looking seedheads like annual opium poppies (*P. somniferum*), so chop off any dead flowers. Once flowering has finished, shear all the stems back to the ground and water the plants to get a fresh new flush of growth. The old foliage quickly becomes brown and ugly, so you need to move quickly, and the second flush can be slow to appear in hot years.

Right: Seeds are the cheapest way to bulk out your garden. Look for colourful annuals such as poppies that you can allow to self-sow around your garden.

How to be a propagating genius

The cheapest way to bulk up a flower garden is to learn how to propagate. Plants have two ways in which they can reproduce, sexually via seeds or asexually by vegetative propagation. These two routes have enabled plants to colonise the world and each method has distinct evolutionary advantages. Sexual reproduction by seed offers an infinite array of genetic variation. It is a plant's way of adapting to an ever-changing environment. However, if plants find themselves in the right conditions then asexual reproduction offers a way to colonise an area very quickly. Many of our worst weeds use vegetative reproduction – couch grass, bindweed, mare's tail and nettles all use tiny fragments of broken roots to take over our gardens.

Vegetative reproduction varies a great deal in plants. Some plants do it through their roots, bulbs or suckers. Some do it with their stems, by layering of rooting stems or stolons (horizontal stem), sometimes called a runner – the humble spider plants produces masses of stolons, each new spider develops on a stolon and will grow to be a separate plant. Others have evolved to reproduce through leaves. Plants have this ability because their cells can differentiate to become a leaf, root or stem very quickly.

A good guide to knowing how a plant will reproduce is to look at its family. For instance, the sage family is easy to identify as they all have square stems; it includes rosemary, salvias, lavender and mint. All readily root from stem cuttings, any stems close to moist soil will produce roots. The stonecrop and houseleek family (Crassulaceae) are all adapted to live in steep, hot, dry rocky places. Many from this family, such as echeverias, crassulas and sedums reproduce from offsets and fallen leaves. If you remove a leaf of an echeveria and put it in very free-draining, gritty soil, it will root, exactly as it would in nature.

Easy propagation

With a bit of practice, anyone can propagate plants by sowing seeds, by dividing clump-forming plants, or by taking cuttings.

You can sow seeds of just about anything, but some will take years to germinate. The only way to propagate annuals and biennials is to sow seed. Annuals live out their entire lives within a season. That means they germinate, flower, set seed and die within a year; for some, their lifespan is a matter of weeks. Most vegetables, many weeds and wild flowers are annuals.

Biennials are a longer versions of annuals; they need two seasons. In the first season they form roots and a rosette of leaves, in the second season they flower, fruit, set seed and die. A common biennial is the foxglove (*Digitalis purpurea*); it forms a rosette of leaves in year one and its flower stalk in year two.

Perennials can live for years and years and most flower every year, although some take a very long time to get round to it. A relative of the pineapple, *Puya raimondii*, takes on average 150 years to flower. All perennials spend the worst season asleep. If a plant doesn't flower and set fruit and die within two seasons, it's a perennial. Trees, bulbs, conifers and woody shrubs are all perennials, but the term is mostly used for herbaceous perennials – non-woody plants that may last anywhere from a few years (short-lived perennial) to decades. Some herbaceous perennials are evergreen, but most drop their leaves and die back to ground level, to leave only the dormant underground roots, rhizomes, bulbs or tubers waiting for the right conditions to come again.

Dividing perennials

Division is the easiest form of propagation for all herbaceous perennials with fibrous roots, such as geraniums and hostas. With a few rare exceptions, you can't divide woody plants.

You simply dig up one plant and pull or ease it apart, or slice it with a spade into several self-supporting ones. You can split a plant many times, but each section must have at least one bud or shoot and its own roots. If a plant is quite small, you can tease it apart by holding the sections just below the bud and pulling gently. This is quick, easy and will yield many small plants. It's a good way to bulk up well-developed, shop-bought plants; just take a perennial, divide and repot each section and wait till they get to a decent size to plant out.

It's generally most useful to divide a plant when it's been growing for a few years, so that each section is a decent size. Nearly all perennials need dividing at some point in their lives in order to keep their growth vigorous. The rule of thumb is to divide every five years or so.

You can divide at any of time of year, but if the weather's hot you'll have more work on your hands. That's why most people choose to divide in autumn or spring, when the plants are dormant and the soil still workable. Irises and spring-flowering plants are best divided in early summer after they've flowered. Plants that flower in early to mid summer are divided in autumn. Late summer- to early autumn-flowering plants are best divided in early spring, before they get going again. This applies to houseplants just the same as to those outdoors.

If your plant is a large beast, such as a huge clump of geranium or a giant pampas grass, teasing it apart with your hands isn't an option. You can split an awful lot with a sharp spade; just hack a section out, making sure you have buds, roots and stems, and throw away any woody bits. For pampas grass and anything with really matted roots, try using a saw. Dig the plant up and saw it into sections. Replant all your divisions into new homes with good compost and water – this should kick-start them into new life.

Opposite page and left: **How to divide a perennial. Fleshy rooted perennials such as this daylily (*Hemerocallis*) can be easily split into sections. This needs to be done roughly every five years to keep plants in good shape.**

Cuttings

Most cuttings are taken from plant stems, but you can also take them from leaves or roots. Some plants want to root so badly that all you need to do is put them in a jar of water and they're off. Mint, coleus, watercress, penstemons, tradescantias and succulent begonias will all root this way. Just take a stem, cut off the lower leaves and make a clean cut across the base with a sharp knife, before putting the stem in a jar of water. Keep the jar topped up to keep the stems submerged and wait two to four weeks. Once the roots appear, pot young plants into good compost and water often for the first couple of weeks while the plant adjusts to its new life.

Other plants need a little more persuasion and you can wait anything from two weeks to four months to get roots. All cuttings taken in late summer need to be protected from the cold over the winter, preferably in a cold frame. Plant them out in spring.

Woody plants

Softwood cuttings are taken from healthy young stems, usually from the first flush of growth in spring. These cuttings root readily, but because they have a lot of green growth they can easily dry out. Softwood cuttings are used to propagate mainly deciduous trees, shrubs and climbers, such as clematis, hydrangeas and deciduous viburnums. These should root in four to six weeks.

A hardwood cutting is taken from something like willow, dogwood, blackberries and flowering currants in late autumn. Look for this year's well-ripened (no longer soft) growth, and take 20cm lengths with a horizontal cut just below the node at the base of each cutting. Cuttings taken in autumn should have rooted by spring.

Nodal, stem tip or soft tip cuttings

It's traditionally recommended to take the tip of the stem as a cutting from perennials or non-woody plants. This is because it contains the powerhouse of new production – both the growing tip and the node where the rooting hormone is produced.

Take cuttings from healthy shoots 8–13cm long. Cut just below a pair of leaves – at the node – with a clean sharp knife, then remove the lowest pair of leaves from your cutting. You do this because in all plants the natural growth hormones congregate at the node, just below a leaf joint. These hormones initiate the new roots. To speed things up you can dip the cuttings in rooting powder.

Your cutting should have no more than one or two sets of leaves, any more will exhaust the new roots. Place cuttings around the edge of a 15cm pot, or in modules, filled with cutting or seed compost. Carefully firm in the cuttings and gently water. Cover the pot or modules with a plastic bag to maintain the humidity, but make sure the bag doesn't touch the cuttings, and keep them out of direct sunlight. Prime examples include pinks and carnations (*Dianthus*), penstemons, Michaelmas daisies, autumn-flowering chrysanthemums and sage (*Salvia*).

Cuttings taken from side shoots on the lower part of a plant usually root better than cuttings taken from higher up. And thinner cuttings root faster than fat ones. Take cuttings early in the morning when plants are turgid, and if you don't have time to pot them straightaway put the cuttings in a freezer bag, seal it and put them in the fridge to deal with later the same day.

Stem or internodal cuttings

Some plants root so readily that it's a shame to limit yourself just to the tip of the stem. Lobelias, asters, phygelius, salvias and penstemons are particularly willing to root, so why take just one cutting per stem when you could have so many more?

The top of a stem cutting should be just above a set of leaves, the base just below a leaf. Each cutting needs to be at least 5–8cm long. Remove the bottom leaves so that you have sufficient length of bare stem to insert into the compost and treat exactly the same way as a nodal cutting. An advantage of internodal cuttings is that they tend to make bushier, better-quality plants.

Leaf cuttings

A limited number of plants can be propagated from leaves; most of these are houseplants such as mother-in-law's tongue (*Sansevieria trifasciata*, see following pages), African violets (*Saintpaulia streptocarpus*) and rex begonias. Leaf cuttings can be taken at any time of year. Most will need to be kept at temperatures between 18–24°C and away from bright sunlight.

Right: **A penstemon stem tip cutting. A good cutting should be 8–13cm long, roughly the length of your thumb. Cut just below a leaf node and remove the lower set of leaves.**

Easy plants to propagate

Division by runners – spider plants and strawberries

Take a baby spider and snip it off the plant. Put some peat-free, multi-purpose compost in a pot, dib a hole about 2.5cm deep in the centre and place the baby spider plant in it. Firm the soil around the spider plant, if it doesn't look secure then you can pin it down with a paperclip bent into a U-shape. Water and place in a warm spot on a windowsill.

Use the same method for strawberry plants and other plants that produce runners. Unlike the spider plant many runners don't develop roots while they're still on the mother plant, so you have to peg the baby plant into a pot while it's still attached. Once it has rooted, usually after a few weeks, cut off the runner close to the new plant.

Leaf cuttings – mother-in-law's tongue (*Sansevieria trifasciata*)

If you thought the spider plant was too easy, this is even better – just cut a mother's tongue leaf into small pieces, put them into soil and they'll grow again. These are called leaf cuttings.

Take a newly mature, healthy leaf and cut it off at the bottom of the plant. Now cut the leaf horizontally into 5cm sections, discarding the tip and the very bottom piece. Insert the cuttings into good potting compost in a seed tray or shallow box. It doesn't matter if the cuttings touch the sides, so cram them in. Keep the compost moist, but not wet, and place the cutting, uncovered, somewhere in bright but indirect light. They like moist warmth – around 21°C – so a warm bathroom is ideal. The important thing is to make sure that all the cuttings are placed the right way up – the way the leaf was growing – rather than upside down. In six to eight weeks, new shoots and roots will appear. Variegated sansevierias – the ones with yellow margins – can be propagated only by division in early spring. If you propagate from leaf cuttings, they'll all come up green.

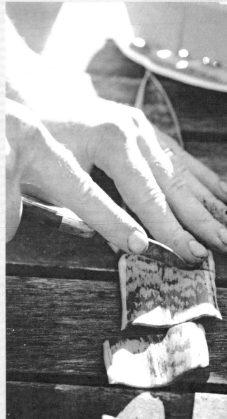

Opposite page and left: **How to take leaf cuttings. Choose a newly mature leaf and slice it into sections, remembering to note which way is up. Then insert the cuttings into a free-draining compost. Keep moist and somewhere sunny and you'll get lots of babies.**

How to root penstemons. Bottom left: Remove any lower sets of leaves. Above: These cuttings are ready to pot on. Top left: Two methods of rooting: water saves on compost if that is a commodity.

Stem-tip and stem cuttings – penstemons

Penstemons are common garden-centre plants as they flower their socks off for much of summer. They are lovely plants from which to start taking stem-tip cuttings, and they root so readily they'll oblige in a jar of water as well as in seed compost. To root them in water, take cuttings 8–13cm long from healthy shoots that aren't too leggy. Trim each cutting just below a set of leaves and remove its lower leaves, to end up with a good portion of the stem in water with a top pair of leaves sitting above the jar. To prevent cuttings falling into the jar, wrap garden wire around the neck or place some wire netting over the jar and insert the cuttings between the wire. Keep the water topped up and, after two to four weeks, you should have lots of well-developed roots. Pot each cutting into an 8cm pot, and water.

To start cuttings in compost, fill a 15cm pot with seed compost and use a chopstick or pencil to make several holes around the edge. Place the cuttings in the holes, gently firm them in and water. Keep the cuttings at the edge of the pot as they like to have a slightly constricted space in which to grow roots. Place a clear bag over the pot, without touching the cuttings, and wait a couple of weeks. Penstemons reproduce just as happily from stem or internodal cuttings, so you can quickly make a whole heap of plants from just one.

For a stem cutting, start with two sets of leaves per cutting. Cut just below the bottom set and remove these leaves. Insert the cutting into the compost as above and cover with a clear plastic bag. These cuttings often produce the best-quality bushy plants. Plants should be ready to pot on in two to four weeks.

Semi-ripe cuttings – carnations and pinks

Known as pipings, semi-ripe cuttings can be taken from pinks (*Dianthus*) successfully from mid to late summer, even from cut flowers although they may struggle in your conditions if they are not from a local grower. Look for a non-flowering shoot, but use a flowering one if nothing else is available. Hold the shoot near the base and pull out the tip, it will break easily at a node. Remove the lowest pair of leaves so that you have about five leaves to a piping and insert into a container of seed or cutting compost. In two to three weeks you'll notice a new flush of growth, a sure sign that the cuttings have rooted. The ideal temperature for rooting pipings is around 15°C. Pot on into individual containers to plant out the following spring.

Heel cuttings – woody plants

Camellias, *Ceanothus* and many semi-woody plants reproduce better if they have a little bit of the stem still hanging on. This is known as the heel. Heel cuttings are also used for plants that are difficult to root. The heel is from an area where there is a natural build-up of rooting hormones so it is the bit that roots. It also helps to prevent against fungal attack.

Carefully pull away a side shoot of this year's growth. Leaves should be healthy, the tip soft, the stem firm and woody at the base with a good green colour. This should be about 10cm long and should come away from the parent shoot with a sliver or 'heel' of bark attached. Trim off the tail of the heel with a sharp knife or secateurs. Remove the lower leaves so you have about 5cm of clear stem to plant into the compost.

Defending your bounty

Wherever there is soil, there'll be weeds. Wherever there are plants, there will be pests, and wherever there are soil and plants, sunshine and rain, you'll probably find diseases. They're all part of gardening, but no-one wants too many weeds, pests or diseases or it can all become a little overwhelming.

Previous page: **Used coffee grounds deter pests such as slugs.** Right: **Dock leaves and dandelions – weeds are the bane of all gardeners.** Opposite page: **Perennial weed soup – ferment beastly weeds in water.**

Weeds and weeding

Weeds are an important part of your garden. Imagine what your compost bin would look like without them? The good news is that weeds show that your soil is alive, and many small creatures make their homes in a weedy patch – you just don't want weeds to take over.

Whatever you do, never let weeds cramp your style. You may never get on top of some, I know that mare's tail will always be a part of my garden, but I've learnt to love its best assets. Weeds are broken down into annuals, which are beastly, and perennials, which are beastly and brutish. The perennials are the real problem. They vanish for the winter, allowing you to believe you've got on top of them, only to appear with the first glimpse of sun.

Why weeds are not welcome

The true definition of a weed is a plant out of place. Most weeds are just wild flowers that have found a niche in your garden soil. Some weeds are plants that you have willingly introduced into your garden. Mint, orache, periwinkle, even hellebores can take over if you don't keep on top of them. The problem with the most common weeds is that they are universally tough. They can continue to grow in conditions where many garden plants give up. This persistence is partly down to robbing the plants around them of moisture, nutrients and sun, which is why you need to get rid of them.

Many weeds act as vectors for pest and diseases, meaning that they either overwinter in the weeds, or use them as a source of food or material, so the more weeds you have the more chance of other unwanted things. And because you don't get to choose where weeds come up, they tend to make a garden look very messy.

Using weeds

The best thing you can do with weeds is to use them to benefit the plants that you do want, by composting them. First you need to recognise your annuals from your perennials. Perennials will make it through even the hottest compost as fragments of root, so you can't put them on your heap as soon as you've weeded them from the ground. Instead soak all perennial weeds, such as bindweed, mare's tail, docks, thistles, yellow-rooted nettles and couch grass, in a bucket with a lid (excluding light makes it decompose quicker). When it's turned into a slimy mass, put this back onto the compost as a nutrient-rich soup. In the winter, it can take several months for the weeds to break down.

If you can't identify a weed, then compost only the green stuff initially and put all the roots and seeds into the soup bucket. This is especially important if your compost doesn't get over 15°C. As well as composting them, you can dig annual weeds back into the soil to act as a source of nitrogen. It's best to do this in spring, when warmer soil temperatures mean the weeds will

decompose quickly. This is a good trick for potatoes; just throw the weeds from the surrounding area into the bottom of the potato trench or hole.

Your heart may sink if you take on a garden smothered in all of the worst weeds. Every book will tell you over and over again that the only truly effective way to get rid of these weeds is to dig. This is true, to some extent. If you're starting from scratch, and if there is nothing in the garden worth keeping, then digging from one end to the other will give you a clean slate – and lose you a few kilos. But it can be a vast undertaking. If this is going to be home for a good long while, then spending the time to get it properly cleared in the first place will pay off, but if you're only going to be there for the next eighteen months or so, is it worth spending several months on the weeds? I don't think so.

The no-dig weeding method

If digging is your idea of hell, you can bypass the whole thing if you are prepared to go and find a lot of cardboard and a good hefty supply of bulky mulch. This isn't an instant solution, but it surely beats weedkiller. If you do find yourself tempted to reach for a bottle of weedkiller, restrain yourself. That's not an instant solution either, and can kill more than the weeds. You weed kill, it looks as though nothing has happened for at least three weeks; then it starts to turn yellow, but this goes on for such a long time that you imagine it might not have worked. You use the weedkiller in late spring, it gets to summer and you want to have a barbecue, but your garden is a very sickly looking yellow. Then suddenly, long after you think anything could possibly happen, all your weeds fall over – and you still have to go and gather them all up. Weedkiller is very effective, but it doesn't work in a hurry and, whatever anyone says, it is not environmentally friendly.

Instead try the cardboard trick. You need lots of cardboard – bike shops are great as they have huge supplies of really large boxes – and lay it down over the weeds. It's best to cut the tops off the weeds first. Cardboard acts as a weed-suppressing membrane and it also rots down. Next cover the cardboard with a thick layer of mulch, at least 15cm. This could be your own compost (but you probably won't have that much), leaf mould, cheap, bought compost, grass clippings, animal bedding, straw, mushroom compost or a mixture of all of them. Use shop-bought stuff as the top layer, whatever else you use, so that your beds look uniform and mulched – rotting cardboard is not a good look. Then all you have to do is wait.

Worms in the soil will go mad for this new layer of food and do all the work for you. The mulch plus the cardboard will suppress the light and the weeds below will be smothered to death. The worms continue doing their thing and if you're patient you can plant straight into a weeded bed. Any weeds that do make it through are easy to pull out. No digging – just a new bed to plant into. This method can be used for everything from establishing a vegetable garden to getting rid of a lawn. If you are doing it in autumn, you can place bulbs such as bluebells and daffodils under the cardboard and nature will do the rest, though if you have squirrels you'll probably have to cover the mulch with chicken wire or they'll dig up all your bulbs.

You may not get rid of some truly persistent perennial weeds, or not with the first attempt. Mare's tail or bindweed for example have roots which seem to have limitless reserves to draw on. However, the no-dig method increases worm activity and so makes

the soil light and workable. If you do have to dig later, at least it won't be backbreaking.

Hitting weeds with mulch

I'm sorry if you have truly persistent weeds, but I mean it when I say don't let them cramp your style – mulch, mulch and mulch again. Apart from Japanese knotweed (contact your council for help or move out – seriously, it's horrible), nearly all other pernicious weeds can be brought into check with mulching. But the mulching has to be deep and regular. The more you mulch, the more organic matter you are slowly adding to your soil. You'll actually see this happening because one day you see lots of mulch and four months later you won't see any. The worms and their friends will have been slowly working it down into your soil. The more organic matter, the more slugs, worms and other munching things appear.

Imagine what happens when weeds have 15cm of mulch dropped on their heads. This makes things very dark, but weeds have some reserves to cope with lack of light so they carry on growing, but they start to struggle and soon some of them begin to rot a little. Along come worms, slugs, mites and, with them, bacteria and moulds and they all start to work on your weeds. By now these are struggling for light, and struggling against attack, and the minute they get their heads out to the sun, you dump more mulch on top of them. Eventually they will give up the struggle.

Most weeds are colonisers of bare, open ground. They may appear when you disturb the ground and expose the weed seed bank that exists in all soil, but they don't actually like disturbed ground per se. As long as you go into this battle armed, you can win!

Left: Cardboard mulching. Top thick cardboard with cheap mulch or home-made compost (bottom). Do this regularly and you'll beat even the most pernicious ones. I use home-made compost and top it off with cheap bark mulch so it looks tidy (top).

Home-made herbicides and other weed deterrents

Gardeners have made their own weed controls for generations, but home-made herbicides and pesticides are illegal under current EU legislation. They are included here only for non-EU gardeners. The most effective home-made weedkiller is a mixture of four cups of vinegar to half a cup of salt and a couple of teaspoons of washing-up liquid. When the salt is fully dissolved, you just spray or wipe it onto broad-leaved weeds such as docks and ground elder. Unfortunately, it's lethal to all other plants around it as well. It works best in sunny conditions. Coca cola is surprisingly good for killing off weeds in pavement cracks. It's a bit sticky, but very effective if used on a sunny day.

But you and your hoe are the best weedkillers out there. If you're out hoeing the tops off annual plants first thing in the morning, the weeds will burn off in the sun. Nothing is more effective. Hoe in dry weather so weeds don't get the chance to regenerate.

Eat your weeds

They used to be part of people's diets, but we now have so much choice we rarely fill our plates with weeds. Eating them into submission is very satisfying. Chickweed is good in salads, not unlike winter purslane, it has a fresh, green taste and can also be used in soups, but you have to pick a whole heap. Ground elder was a Roman treat as its pernicious nature meant it was around even in winter. You eat it a bit like spinach, picking only the young leaves and gradually exhausting the plant. Fat hen is a medieval herb used, unsurprisingly, to fatten hens. It's a big, thirsty annual that looks a bit like dock but tastes good enough in salads or stemmed like spinach. Stinging nettles are packed full of vitamin C and young leaves make a delicious spring soup. Young dandelion leaves are very good for indigestion – slightly bitter but a good addition to salads and very tasty sautéed.

Japanese knotweed is enough to send most gardeners weeping, but sautéeing, steaming or simmering the young shoots is one sort of revenge. They have a slightly tart taste which is like either asparagus or rhubarb, depending on whom you speak to. Choose young shoots 15–20cm long, and discard any leaves, as these are too tough.

Perennial beasts

Mare's tail	Japanese knotweed – you might want to consider moving to a different home... But seriously, you'll need a two-pronged attack. Pull up or cut the extensive root system every time you see a shoot appearing; over several years this will exhaust the root system. Every shoot or root will need to be dried out thoroughly before being disposed of. Never put any part into the water system. You can also spot-treat individual plants with a glyphosate-based herbicide. It will still take several years to clear the ground.
Bindweed	
Couch grass	
Creeping buttercup	
Creeping thistle	
Ground elder	
Dock	
Bramble	
Buddleja	
Bracken	
Ground ivy	

Left: Eat your weeds. Yes, I ate my weeds – chickweed and dandelion salad. The good things about many weeds is they grow in winter. So one way to look at them is as a source of winter greens.

Pest and disease control

No sooner have you started to get to grips with weeds than you may start noticing some other things you didn't invite into your garden. Just as where there is bare soil there'll be weeds, where there are plants you like (and some you don't), there will be pests and other things to mar your work.

This may sound tough, but it's not the end of the world. The very words 'pests and diseases' make them sound utterly unwanted and horrible, but they do have reasons to be here. They are all part of this ecosystem called life and important for that reason. Slugs, for instance, are horrible to look at and destroy countless lovely things with what seems like insider knowledge of what matters most to you. But they also play an important part in breaking down organic matter. When the earth produces so much organic matter, why are we not drowning in it? Think about it. The reason the earth's surface isn't getting larger year on year is because there are things like worms, slugs, fruit flies, land snails, nematodes and all sorts of other bugs working hard to turn waste vegetable matter into soil. A lot of plant diseases also break down plant material to put it back into the soil. These things are here for a reason.

Our gardens are manufactured environments where certain things do a little too well. We do our best to make sure we have good soil, plenty of water and lots of good, rich growth – wouldn't you want to move in? However, I'm not suggesting that we embrace each snail or spider mite with open arms. When you've spent month raising a tomato plant or row of tasty carrots, it's hard not to become completely irrational when something starts attacking it. I think there is a little bit of warfare inside most people and bugs make easy prey. It's fine to go on a killing spree, as long as you do it with the lives of others in mind. This means staying clear of pesticides.

Why not use pesticides?

The problem is that, on the whole, they are indiscriminate. If you look on the back of a pesticide container, more often than not that it will say in small print somewhere that it will harm bees and aquatic life. It's saying that this product will kill your pests, but it will kill the good bugs along with the bad.

Insects are the bottom of the food pyramid, which means there need to be huge numbers of them to attract relatively small numbers of the wildlife you love, such as song birds, birds of prey or cute small mammals.

Go organic

If you go organic you have to – begrudgingly at times – get on with living with everything. When you want to get rid of a pest or disease, you'll have to do it pest by pest rather than in one sweeping spray. You can hand pick or squish a lot of unwanted insects, such as caterpillars. It does take time, but it's not an impossible job. Another method is to blast insects with a jet of water, but not so hard as to damage leaves. This will dislodge many undesirables. Clearing away dead or dying leaves that may harbour diseases, planting nectar-rich flowers for pollinators amongst your veg, and generally keeping things clean, paths swept and pots washed goes a long way towards keeping down pests and diseases.

Organic methods rely on good husbandry, prevention and healthy soil. As a fully paid-up member of this crew, I can testify hand on heart that healthy soil really does mean less problems.

Visible thugs

Organic gardeners just have to accept the unwanted side-kicks that are slugs and snails. They love soil rich in organic matter. There are lots of different slugs out there: usually the smaller they are, the more damage they do. My mantra is big and black – put it back (in the compost bin where it will help make compost), but if it's brown – as well as orange, tiger-striped or yellowish – smash it down.

All snails are after your plants. Snails are more desirable to predators than slugs as they taste better so they do attract some birds and, in fact, if you're feeling brave you can eat the common garden snail. Collect some, put them in a bucket and feed them on carrots until their poo turns orange, then sauté them in garlic and white wine.

Aphids are a major annoyance in most gardens. Greenfly, whitefly, blackfly, mealy and root aphids are all small insects that suck sap, causing physical damage and transmitting viruses. They also shit constantly because they're always munching in order to get enough protein, so they excrete a sticky substance called honeydew all over the leaves, which in turn grows black sooty mould and attracts other pests. Caterpillars are the larval forms of moths and butterflies and they just love to dine on plants, particularly brassicas. The good thing is that they are very easy to spot.

Soil pests

Chafer grubs, leatherjackets and cutworms are all revolting to look at. Chafers are white, leatherjackets are earth-coloured and cutworms are greenish grey. All look utterly unappealing and eat either plants' roots or their stems at soil level.

Indoor pests

Aphids, glasshouse whitefly, red spider mite, scale insects and mealy bugs all love warm conditions. Aphids and whitefly are pretty easy to spot. Red spider mites are tiny, tiny things. Lots of them tend to cause a yellow mottling on the topside of the leaf; when you look at the underside there is a fine web and, with careful eyesight, you can see tiny red mites running about.

Scale insects are immobile, usually round and the colour of light brown paper. If you take your nail to them, you can flick off the brown papery outside and see a squishy insect inside. Once you've flicked its cover off, it dies. Mealy bugs are covered in a white powdery coating and are closely related to scale insects, except they move very slowly. You can use methylated spirits to zap them (not an approved organic method), which is really fun as they go from white to bright red and fall off. I know it's childish, but it's satisfying. Otherwise, give your indoor plants a good clean with a rag and soapy water every so often and you'll get rid of a great deal.

Fungal diseases

Moulds and mildews are caused by fungi, with downy and powdery mildew the most common. You can easily tell them apart as powdery mildew appears on both the upper and lower leaf surfaces and the plant looks as if it has been dusted in flour. Powdery mildew likes high humidity and warm temperatures, so you'll find it in spring and autumn. It's best to prune out infected material and don't compost it. Choose resistant varieties and make sure that they are adequately spaced as poor air circulation leads to mildew build-up.

Downy mildew only occurs on the undersides of leaves, the topsides of the leaves will have yellow blotches. It's often bad in wet summers, when the weather is relatively cool and very humid. Again, air circulation is very important in deterring downy

Right: Encourage wildlife to eat your pests. Plants such as these sunflowers (*Helianthus annuus*) will attract beneficial insects such as hoverflies and insectivorous birds into your garden on the hunt for pollen and seeds. In return, they'll eat your aphids.

mildew. Plants in shady corners tend to get hit so look for disease-resistant plants or varieties. Bee balsam (*Monarda*), peas, lettuces, vines and roses are all very susceptible to mildews.

Good husbandry

Good hygiene is an important strategy in your battle against pests and diseases. Plant debris is a key home for many nasties, and general garden rubbish such as old plant pots are ideal breeding grounds for slugs and snails. Many weeds also act as homes for diseases or places to lay eggs. The more you weed, the less homes you provide.

Good practice is the other weapon. Some cultural practices discourage diseases and pests from hanging around or moving in. When you rotate your vegetables this means the soil pests that prefer specific families of plants are starved of their favourite hosts. For example, never grow onions in the same bed as you've grown leeks the year before.

Give your plants the best chance by growing them in good conditions. Seedlings that start life in poor soil conditions will be stressed and susceptible to attack, so never sow in very cold or wet or very dry soil. Thin them early to avoid overcrowding – fungal diseases are most likely to spread where plants are too close.

Companion planting

Companion planting means planting specific combinations together for good health. The idea is that a monoculture is asking for trouble, but interplanting with certain flowers and vegetables can deter and confuse pests. French marigolds (*Tagetes patula*) between tomatoes and peppers prevent whitefly attacks because marigold roots release a substance disliked by whitefly. Plant nasturtiums next to cabbages and you may divert many caterpillars onto these as they are very partial to nasturtiums. If you plant clover (*Trifolium* ssp.) as a cover crop under brassicas, pests that want to lay their eggs in the soil will have a hard time finding it because of the dense clover. The onion family is known to repel aphids, whitefly and carrot fly, and for this reason onions, garlic and chives are often planted next to carrots, tomatoes, peppers and brassicas.

At the very least, it's a good idea to have lots of nectar-rich flowers growing beside your vegetables. Poached egg plants, marigolds, sunflowers, fennel and thyme act as nectar and pollen sources for beneficial insects. Birds, hoverflies, ladybirds, spiders, ground beetles, devil's coachmen (big black beetles that eat slugs) and lacewings are all hungry for pests, especially for aphids. Work on the principle that if it's moving fairly fast, then it hunts prey and is good; the plant-eaters that you don't want tend to be slow movers. Frogs, toads, ducks and hedgehogs make light work of slugs and snails. Many wasps are parasitic on pests and should be encouraged, not swatted.

A few chemicals are allowed under organic principles. These chemicals tend to be non-toxic to the soil, break down quickly and do not kill everything else in their wake. All organic chemicals work as contact poisons, which mean they don't hang around, but it also means they to have to be used more often. Horticultural soaps containing fatty acids are used to kill aphids and other sap-sucking insects. Sulphur dust is used to treat powdery mildews. Always stick to the manufacturers' instructions and always dispose of chemical bottles responsibly. Spray in the evening when beneficial insects tend not to be around, and don't get anywhere near water sources.

I'm really only happy to use diluted horticultural soap in my garden. This is a soft soap spray based on fatty acids. It blocks the spiracles – the breathing holes – on insects and is effective against aphids, whitefly and red spider mite. But it will also harm beneficial insects, so you need to be selective. By using a hand spray, you can be pretty accurate with what you drown. A weak solution of biodegradable washing-up liquid, no more than a couple of squirts into a spray bottle, works just the same as horticultural soap. Never spray in full sun, or the liquid can scorch your plants.

Pyrethrum is another pesticide you often see advertised as appropriate for organic gardeners. It is made from a plant extract from a type of chrysanthemum and is particularly effective against aphids, whitefly and red spider mite. It is also non-selective, so will harm beneficial insects. Many organic gardeners, including me, don't use it for ethical reasons because its production in the developing world hasn't had a great track record.

Slug pellets developed for organic gardeners are based on ferric phosphate. As a last resort, if you are overrun with slugs and snails, they can be very effective.

Left and opposite page: **Mixing your flowers and your vegetables really does work. Marigolds (left) will attract masses of predatory insects, such as wasps and hoverflies. Nasturtiums (opposite) will encourage pollinators and also lure cabbage white butterflies away from your brassicas.**

Right: These plants have been ravaged by slugs, but the copper ring, which I found in a skip, should deter any newcomers, giving them a fighting chance to come back.

Opposite page: Sawdust is a very effective slug deterrent in dry weather.

pest controls

Slugs hate copper. When their slime touches copper, it gives them an electric shock. Keep a look out in skips for any pieces of copper pipe and bend it into rings to place around precious plants.

Slugs hate coffee. Their feet get irritated by all the caffeine so they start to produce lots of slime; this dehydrates them and eventually kills them. Spent coffee from your local coffee shops does the trick. Spread it wide and thin for the best effect, and it's a good plan to spread it over seed rows before seedlings emerge.

Slugs hate sawdust. It dehydrates them, so they move off it. They hate soot for the same reason, and crushed eggshells.

Slugs hate salt. If you're really annoyed by them, pour it on and watch them fizz.

Slugs love beer. Cut a plastic bottle in half and sink the bottom half into the ground. Pour in old slops from your local bar and cover with a plant pot to stop beneficial beetles and other creatures from falling in. Slugs clamber in, get drunk and drown. It's very effective, but you need lots of traps. Fruit juice can be substituted for beer, but they would rather drink beer.

Carrot fly can be a real pest, but barriers will help as the insects don't fly above 60cm. Thinning young carrots early also helps.

A milky solution sprayed onto plants will discourage mildews by making the leaf surfaces more alkaline, which mildews can't tolerate.

Red spider mite can be easily discouraged with water. The mites thrive in dry conditions, so regularly spray infected material with water, making sure to saturate the undersides of the leaves.

If your houseplants are covered in little bugs, give them a good shower to wash off an awful lot of baddies, and be sure to wash the top of the pot and under the rim.

The
harvest

Autumn preparation

You plant and grow, sow and dig, you weed and clear, you stake, support, marvel and pick. Some days are amazing, some may be heart-breaking, it's all go… and then just like that it comes to a rapid end. Summer ends, perhaps lingering a little, but suddenly it's time to move rapidly. Your work doesn't stop when your main growing season is over. What you pick, bottle and store now will give you comfort and pride over the coming months, and tidying up in autumn means you don't have to go out when the weather's really foul – unless you want to.

Cherish good days in autumn. It often starts bright and sunny, but as winter draws on it's sure to get cold and cheerless. Once you've harvested all you can, it's time to put your garden to bed. Remove leaves from lawns and beds and put them in a sack or a chicken-wire frame to turn into leaf mould. Cut back dead foliage and most stems on herbaceous perennials, but leave attractive seedheads and a few spent stems standing for insects to sleep in through the winter. Clean bird baths and bring in any houseplants that spent summer outside. If your worm bin lives outside or in a shed, wrap it up to keep the worms warm and active.

Cover outdoor containers filled with winter salads and greens with horticultural fleece or bubble wrap. Olives, bays, tender palms, dahlia tubers, canna lilies, gingers (*Hedychium*) and bananas will all need to be protected for the winter in all but the mildest climate. Wrap olives, bays and other tender perennials in bubble wrap or fleece. If they are in pots, stand them on bits of polystyrene to stop the cold creeping up from the ground – the polystyrene bases from frozen pizzas will suffice. Dahlia tubers can be left in the ground as long as it doesn't freeze all winter or get too wet. I mulch on top of these and other tender bulbs and tubers once the foliage has died back with a good 15cm of mulch, then cover with old compost bags, which I pin down to stop the worst of the rain. I wrap bananas in chicken wire and straw, although I've seen unprotected ones get through pretty tough weather.

Autumn is a good time to move any plants that are in the wrong place as the soil is workable and most things are going into dormancy, but you can still see where they are. Autumn is also the time to plant spring-flowering bulbs; as you clear spent foliage and cut back your perennials, make use of the bare soil you uncover to pop in as many tulips as you can.

Left: A tidy up in autumn gives you a chance to take stock of things, move plants and collect seeds. Don't be too tidy, attractive seedheads, such as those of grasses, provide interest over winter.

Saving your own seed

An obvious reason to save seed is to save money – why buy new seed when you can harvest your own? But actually there is a lot more to it than thrift. In the last 40 years or so, gardeners have gone from being prolific seed savers to enthusiastic purchasers of commercial seeds. Most seeds on sale are hybrids, where every seed is the same, year after year, rather than traditional open-pollinated varieties (see Growing Heirloom Varieties on p. 92). There is nothing wrong with buying seed, you have to start somewhere, but it is genuinely important to save your own.

When you save open-pollinated seed from your own garden, you are maintaining slightly different strains of vegetables and flowers. These strains represent a living gene bank that is adapted to local conditions. Every seed is a little bit different and widely adapted and adaptable to different conditions. For instance, if you grow from seed from an heirloom tomato (check it's open-pollinated) you bought from a market and then save your seed, that tomato is already showing signs of adaptation to your conditions.

Commercial hybrid seed is identical in every packet, every year. This means that growers have to adapt their growing conditions to the seed, not the other way round. We have unwittingly created a standardised growing system, which relies on standard conditions and fertilisers. Yet our climate has never been, and never will be, constant. We need a gene bank that will have enough variation to adapt to our future needs. Seed saving is fun, cheap and a powerful political gesture.

Collecting seed is easy. You just need a little botany, some paper bags, a pencil and the willingness to give up part of your fridge to next year's bounty.

Seed forms as a result of pollination and successful fertilisation of a flower. Pollination can occur through wind, insects or animals. Once it happens, an embryo begins to form. This contains cells that will develop into the first root, stem and eventually leaves. All of this is bundled together and wrapped up in a seed coat. The seed coat is there to protect the contents of the seed, not only from physical harm, but also environmental. It's the seed coat that prevents the seed from germinating in the wrong conditions.

On top of the seed coat, some seeds are also protected by fleshy tissue, such as fruits and hips. This tissue is usually there to entice an animal to take the seed elsewhere, so it has the chance to colonise new territory. Some seed is contained within capsules that delay seed dispersal until the seed is ripe.

Opposite page: The best time to harvest seed is when they are ripe on the plant. This tends to be autumn for most summer-flowering plants. From top left, clockwise: Seedheads and pods of California poppies, chillies, marigolds, sunflowers (seedhead and flowers), love-in-the-mist. Centre: Hollyhock seeds.

Think of the way a poppy seedhead doesn't open its apertures until the seed is ready to go. Catching your seed to save at the right moment of ripeness is essential, too immature and it won't have set itself up for life. A general indicator is that the seed has darkened and hardened.

Most plants in your garden set seed at the end of the growing season, usually in autumn. This makes sense in terms of growing, but also poses a dilemma. This is the time of year when temperatures are lowering, persistent rain, frost and snow are all to come. Clearly, this is not a wise time to germinate, hence the seed coat. The harder and tougher the seed coat, the more the plant is attempting to protect the

seed from germinating at the wrong time, and the longer the seed will last. Tough seed coats are often impervious to water and need to soak in water before germination occurs. Think of a bean or pea – once the seed coat has softened with spring rain the seed can spring into action. The architecture of the seed needs time to develop.

How to collect and store seed

Some seeds, such as cowslips (*Primula veris*), need to be sown ripe for good germination, but most seed needs to be dried thoroughly. Wet seed rots, goes mouldy and quickly becomes unviable.

If you time seed collecting right, nature will have dried your seed for you. But timing is everything: dry seed is quick to fall to the ground or off on to the wind, so you have to catch it just right. In some instances, particularly with perennials, it's better to take the whole seedhead off and dry the seed inside so that you don't lose any by missing the right moment. In a wet year you'll need to take whole heads inside, for example chop all your opium poppies down and take them indoors before they are fully ripe, otherwise the heads will just rot. Hang these upside down over a bucket and the aperture will slowly open over a number of days to release the seed.

Ideally, you should collect all seed in paper bags as these will allow your seed to continue to dry. If you're collecting seed when you're out walking, just make a little paper wrap as this will allow the seeds to breathe.

Left: **Sweet pea seeds – you can tell when they are ready for picking as the pod splits open.** Opposite page: **Brambles – botanical rambles and their finds. Seed wraps from foraging in other people's gardens.**

Cleaning and storing seed

Seeds may need cleaning before you can store them.
From pine cones to pumpkins, nature has developed
different fruiting bodies to protect unfertilised seeds
and aid dispersal of ripe ones. Some seeds require little
cleaning other than teasing off chaff. Others are a little
more involved.

All clean, dried seed should be stored in containers,
either sealed and labelled paper packets or old film
canisters, small Tupperware or used plastic tubs with
lids all work fine. If you've stored everything in
envelopes or paper wraps, you should then put them
into a plastic box with a lid, as airtight conditions are
important. Store in the fridge at a temperature of
1–5°C. If you don't have space in your fridge, store
your seed somewhere consistently dry and cool –
warm, humid conditions kill seed pretty quickly.

Wet seed

To clean seed from fleshy fruit, such as melons or
pumpkins, scoop as much seed from the flesh as
possible into a sieve. Using the back of a spoon, rub
the seed into the sieve under running water until the
flesh starts to come off. Once you've removed as much
as possible spread the seeds out on kitchen paper and
let them dry before storing them.

To get seed from most berries, simply put them into
a fine sieve and squash them under running water until

Above and right: Cleaning up tomato seeds. Remove the bulk of the pulp under running water (right) and then put the seeds into a glass with water and soda crystals (above). The good seed sinks and the bad seed floats.

they are well mashed. Then put the fruit pulp into a jar of water and let it settle. The viable seed will sink and the flesh will float. Carefully pour out the liquid so the seed stays in the jar. Dry the seed on kitchen paper and store it.

Tomato seeds are surrounded by gelatinous gloop that is there to inhibit the seed from germinating in the tomato. This needs to be removed. You can ferment the seeds to clean them, but this method stinks and takes several days. I prefer a method that isn't organically approved, but far quicker. Cut your tomato in half and scoop out the seeds. Wash off the bulk of the jelly in a sieve. Put the seeds in a glass of water (roughly 250ml) and squirt in some washing-up liquid, or a sprinkling of soda crystals. Leave this overnight. Viable tomato seeds will sink to the bottom, but immature seeds will float. Scoop out any immature seeds and then strain the good seeds through a fine sieve. Leave the seeds to dry on coffee filter paper or a china plate – don't use kitchen paper, as you'll never get the little seeds unstuck. When dry store tomato seeds in an airtight container in the fridge or a cool place.

Damp seed

As usual, to every rule there's an exception, and some seeds should not be allowed to dry out. Generally, large oily seeds such as acorns, walnuts and magnolia seeds need to be stored damp. If they dry out, they lose their ability to take up water again. Store this seed in vermiculite in a sealed plastic bag in the fridge.

Dry seed

If possible, collect dry seed from seed capsules on a dry day. Some seed is easy. For columbines, love-in-the-mist, poppies and foxgloves, just tip, shake or split the capsule onto a piece of paper and collect the seed. Smaller, finer seed that is harder to extract can be rubbed through a fine sieve over a piece of paper. A lot of the finer seed from the daisy family Asteraceae, thistle-forming seedheads and lettuce seed can be cleaned this way. If you gently break up the seedhead, the seeds will fall through the sieve, leaving the chaff behind.

A note on cross-pollination

Maybe your lovely garden has lots of pumpkins and they are all different varieties happily growing together. If you decide to collect seed, some cross-pollination (or hybridisation) is bound to have occurred. Pollination occurs when the male pollen from one flower is taken to the female stigma of a different one. The bees, animals or wind that pollinate your plants don't care what variety it is. And the plants care even less about keeping their names pure, they're just on a mission for the next generation. Left alone, pink hellebores don't always produce pink hellebores, yellow courgettes may not produce yellow courgettes. Nature isn't interested in keeping specific strains true, that's down to humans. In some plants it can take a lot of work; you have to hand-pollinate flowers and then protect each one from visits by any other would-be pollinators by covering its head with a bag.

There's no reason why you shouldn't collect cross-pollinated seed. DIY hybridising has been going on for years and is an established method for finding new varieties. Just remember that if you want to get exactly the same plant again, you'll have to isolate its flowers from the attentions of unwanted visitors.

Dealing with gluts

Usually your harvest each year determines what you'll plant next year. Too much or too little is to a degree determined by a year's weather conditions, but it also highlights whether you sowed the right amount to start with. Remember that successional sowing – when you sow roughly every two weeks – of fast-growing crops is a good way of making sure you have a continuous and manageable supply.

Some gluts are lovely, it's hard to imagine you could ever have too many tomatoes, but others are testing. The first French beans are delicious, and the second lot, and the third, and suddenly you can't pick them quick enough and they get stringy. My best tip is to go thrifting for some 1970s veg books. The height of the self-sufficiency movement meant dozens of books on how to bottle, freeze and curry your way out of a glut.

Preserving herbs

Fresh herbs are wonderful, but you can't keep tender herbs such as basil growing through the winter, so at some point you'll have to bottle, dry and harvest.

A small bunch of herbs added to a bottle of oil or vinegar will give it a delicate fragrance and you'll capture summer all year round. I tend to pick basils and rosemary towards the end of the summer, early in the morning when they are at their freshest. For strong herbs such as rosemary, add a pinch of salt or some peppercorns with the herbs, and leave the oil or vinegar for several weeks to absorb the flavour.

Deep-freezing herbs is the least hassle of all and preserves their natural flavours well. Collect and clean bunches of herbs with their stems on. Dip them into boiling water first if you want to keep their colour, pat them dry and spread them loosely in freezer bags. You don't even have to chop them up as they'll be brittle when you take them out, so you can just rub them

into your dish. Basil nearly always goes black in the freezer, it doesn't change the taste, but just doesn't look so pretty. If colour is important to your dish, whizz the basil up in a blender, add a good amount of oil to make a paste and freeze. It's a pared-down pesto that tastes great – store in ice-cube trays for convenience.

Drying herbs

Air drying literally means hanging the herbs upside down in a warm, dry, dark room. Depending on the thickness of the stems and leaves you are drying, this can take anything from a couple of days to a couple of weeks. The herbs are dry when they feel like paper to touch and crumble gently under pressure. All dried herbs should be stored in airtight containers and out of direct light.

Oven drying

You can oven dry your herbs on racks as long as you dry them very slowly over several hours – with a gas oven, just the pilot light should do the trick.

Harvesting flowers for drying

Drying flowers is a lovely thing to do. I'm not a huge fan of pot-pourri, it's a little too grannyish, but a big bunch of dried roses or hydrangeas in the corner of a room can look lovely. Also lots of seedheads, such as opium poppies, love-in-the-mist and giant cardoons, all look great in vases or tied upside down for a rustic look. There are a few basic rules. Heat and moisture determines a lot when you're drying flowers. If you want them to keep their colour, just hang them upside down somewhere with a constant temperature, preferably not too humid and out of direct sunlight. You need space to do this on a large scale, so for starters, try something easy like lavender or roses.

Left: Dried herbs. This is one of my favourite mixes. Dry bay, thyme, rosemary, sage, chillies and garlic cloves very slowly and then crumble everything together to create a Mediterranean seasoning.

163

Herbal teas

If you're short of space and time for gardening, I think you can't do better than grow herbs to harvest for tea. Going out into your garden on a sunny morning and picking your morning brew is a heavenly experience. And storing enough to get you through the winter is very satisfying. Many of our favourite herb teas including mint, camomile and lemon verbena are not only happy in containers, but pretty too.

Making herbal teas

You will need one tablespoon of dried or two of fresh herbs per person, though clearly taste will vary and you can get away with far less of strong herbs like rosemary or lemon verbena. Pour the hot water onto the herbs and steep for at least five minutes. Most herbs drop to the bottom of the cup as they absorb water, but very dry herbs tend to float, so straining in some cases is necessary. If you like sweet tea, then sweeten with honey rather than sugar as that somehow tastes wrong with subtle herbs.

Camomile is always best used dry rather than fresh for tea. I find two or three plants is sufficient supply for two people drinking the occasional cup. For those with an addiction, you need to grow about ten plants. Cut camomile in late summer when the plant is in full flower, cutting the whole stem at ground level, and dry the plant upside down somewhere cool, dark and dry. This takes one to two weeks. Remove only the flower heads for tea, and store them in a cool cupboard in an airtight container.

Feverfew tea is ideal for headaches. It works wonders but tastes bitter – a little honey makes for a much more pleasing tea. Lemon balm soothes sore stomachs. Tea made from the leaves has a pleasant lemony taste and you can drink it in great quantities, which is just as well because it's a rampant plant so it's best grown in pots where it'll stand any amount of abuse. If you cut stems back in June, you'll have tender leaves for the rest of the summer.

Lemon verbena is one of my favourites. It's a delicate, beautiful shrub with lovely white flowers and lemon verbena tea is like lemon boiled sweets, honey and tart all at once. Perfect in a container, it is semi-evergreen and can be pruned back hard in spring for a new flush of leaves. Bring it inside in the winter as it hates very wet or cold conditions.

There are dozens of different mints. Black-stemmed *Mentha piperita* is a good one for tea. *Mentha longifolia* subsp. *schimperi* is a Moroccan mint with a strong peppermint flavour and it is worth investing in to make the traditional Moroccan tea, very concentrated and boiled up with lots of sugar. Unlike others, this variety needs full sun so is a good choice for a pot on a hot patio. Other mints aren't generally much good in tea and eau-de-cologne mint (*Mentha* x *piperita* f. *citrata*) is positively unpleasant but lovely in baths or dried and stuffed into pillows.

Some garden teas are more than pleasing, they're home-grown medicine. If you can get over the taste of stuffing, rosemary, hyssop and sage are really good for sore throats. The minute you feel your throat catching, nip out into the garden, pick fresh herbs and steep them for a short while. Rosemary and sage are both strong tastes, so you can add lemon to make it more palatable. Another variation is to boil honey, lemon, garlic, rosemary, hyssop and sage and then let the mixture steep as long as possible.

Opposite page: **Herbal cuppas, clockwise from top left. Calming camomile, cool mint sun tea, hot apple mint tea, rosehips, for vitamin C, together with feverfew for sore heads, growing at the base.**

Under the radar

Tools of the trade

You need certain things to make your own world. Tools and materials are essential, but finding the right community to bounce ideas off is as much part of thrifty gardening as finding a great watering can in a skip. Once you start gardening, you're sure to find like-minded people, and you don't need to spend a fortune. There are great finds to be had second hand, in skips and online.

Every thrifty gardener needs tools for craft and building projects, but what you need first and foremost are your gardening tools. Don't get lured into buying silly tools. 'Makes digging really easy', 'The no-bend method', Anything that claims to pull out specific weeds, along with tools that look more like torture instruments, are all generally useless and will just sit around instead of being used. Do spend money on a few good tools, the best you can afford. Or get the best you can find in second hand shops and stalls – make sure that metal parts are in good shape, but you can get wooden handles replaced by good ironmongers if needs be.

For gardening in the ground, your most important tool is a good spade, preferably with a wooden handle and a stainless-steel head. The handle should come up to your hip. Digging is hard work and a wooden handle shouldn't jar your bones while many man-made ones can't help it. Look for hickory or oak. A good fork is also a good investment; wooden-handled is best, but you can get away with plastic as forkwork tends to be much less jarring than digging. A hoe, on the other hand, can be as cheap as anything – just make sure the handle is well secured to the blade.

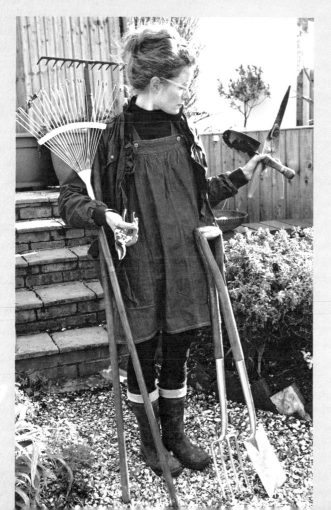

Left: **A few of my favourite things – Mrs Frankfort's tools. I inherited this lot from Mrs Frankfort, a lovely old lady I used to garden for. The narrow rake is a landscaping one, the broad one's a springbok.**
Opposite page: **These letters came from a skip outside my local pub, together with a huge ampersand, which I have no idea what to do with.**

A pair of secateurs is vital. Secateurs have a habit of hiding or disappearing, so buy the cheapest, strongest-looking pair you see. You also need a good, strong pair of scissors. If you lose secateurs, you'll probably lose hand forks and trowels, so get cheap ones. It may seem strange, but you'll find you need several different rakes. Start off with at least one size of hard landscaping rake, used for breaking up soil and creating seedbeds, and one springbok for raking leaves. Spend money here to make sure the rake and handle actually stay together, cheap ones can fall apart far too easily.

If you've got space you'll need a barrow. The cheapest ones are builder's barrows. You often see them in skips at the end of a job covered in plaster – not pretty, but still functional. Horticultural barrows have higher sides, so are more useful – that's the sort of thing I'd put on my Christmas wish list rather than buying myself. Tub trugs are a great invention – large, wide plastic buckets with two handles.

A watering can is essential. I like very old-fashioned metal ones, but a cheap pound-store version will work just as well. A good watering rose is essential and these can be flimsy on cheap versions, so shop around.

Container gardeners need a hand trowel and hand fork, and a hand rake is surprisingly useful for making a seedbed. Secateurs are a good investment, but a sturdy strong pair of scissors can do the job too.

Cheap or free extras

You need something to make holes in the soil or compost for planting seedlings and small bulbs. You can buy custom-made dibbers, but it's fine to use pencils, take-away chopsticks or spoon handles. White plastic plant labels can be cleaned and reused very easily; with thrift, one pack can last a long time. Use wire wool to clean off any writing. It's always best to write in pencil rather than felt pen, as graphite doesn't degrade. Use clear nail varnish to stop the writing fading.

Yogurt pots, take-away trays and old Tupperware pots can all be used as growing containers for seeds and cuttings – poke drainage holes in the bottom. It's easiest to sow seeds in straight lines in most vegetable beds: make a garden line to mark out seed drills from short sections of bamboo canes or bits of wood and string. Large plastic bottles can be quickly made into cloches to keep the frost off vulnerable seedlings. Just chop the bottom off and stick the top over a seedling.

Old ways

This is the most granny thing I've ever told anyone, but kneeling pads are really useful, so make yourself a grantastic DIY one by taking an old hot water bottle, three quarters fill it with sand, and kneel on it.

If your hands have the kind of permadirt that looks as if it may never come off, mix up a gritty paste of sugar and washing-up liquid. Rub this vigorously into your hands and wash it off. Then dry your hands and rub them together with a second mixture of sugar and olive oil for as long as you can be bothered. The sugar will slough off dead skin and the olive oil nourishes it.

Essential tool kit

It took me a long time to realise that tools other than the gardening sort can be really good fun. The reason was that it took me that long to meet a friendly instructor. In my experience, this is not your partner, particularly if they complain about your driving skills. So find someone you are never going to go to bed with and ask them to show you how to use tools.

Power tools are great because they really do save time and energy. Electric drills are not expensive, but it's worth spending time researching brands. In my opinion, only the high-end cordless drills are worthwhile and they're not cheap, so better to buy a mid-price corded drill and a long extension lead as your money will go further. Corded drills tend to be more powerful and go faster than cordless models.

Sanders are also worth investing in. A basic hand-held multi-sander, with an interchangeable base for different jobs, is the best buy. It will tackle any DIY job from removing paint on a rounded chair leg to smoothing a table top.

Electric drills

There is one simple but essential rule to using an electric drill, and that is that you must drill straight or else you snap the drill bit in half. The only other common problems are to do with the settings. If the drill shudders as you're drilling this means you either have it on too low a setting or you have it on the screwdriver setting. The other thing to remember is to turn the power down when you use the drill as a screwdriver or else you strip the screw.

You use different bits depending on what material you're drilling into. Bits are measured in millimetres and you should aim to use a bit that is slightly smaller than your screw. If you use the same size or slightly larger, the screw has nothing to bite into. Wood bits

have a sharp point at the end that allows the drill to bite into the wood. Mortar bits look like miniature hammerhead sharks and should never be used on wood. HSS bits (stands for high speed steel) can be used on plastic, wood and metal. They are usually brass-coloured with flat heads and drill slower than a wood bit, but are stronger and less likely to snap.

Sanders

These are fantastic for tidying mistakes. If you get a lot of wood out of the skip, you'll need to remove glue, plaster and paint and one of the quickest ways is with a sander. Once a piece of sandpaper is worn out, replace it. Always start with the roughest sandpaper (60), then medium (80) and finally fine (120). Probably the most useful is a multi-sander that will do a variety of jobs.

Whatever any sander says about having a system for catching the dust, it's rubbish. Basically they blow dust all over the place, so it's best to do projects outside if possible. Slugs hate trying to crawl over woodshavings so save these to scatter round precious plants, at the very least put them in the compost.

Hand tools

Having a good saw and knowing how to use it is incredibly useful. There's more to a saw handle than meets the eyes; the long bit that attaches to the blade can be used to measure a right angle; the slanting bit to measure a 45 degree cut needed to make a mitre joint such as the corner of a picture frame. If you want to draw a straight line you place the handle on the horizontal part of your wood and slot it into place, this gives you a perfect right angle.

In order to cut a straight line, you must draw a cutting line, otherwise you will never get it straight. Draw the cutting line on both the vertical and horizontal surface of the wood, then saw to the outside of the line. If you don't have a workbench you'll need to clamp the wood to something with a G-clamp. If you don't have a clamp, rest the wood on a chair and place your knee on the wood to keep it in place.

Make sure you're holding the piece of wood at the opposite end to the clamp or else the wood will fall onto your feet and you'll end up with the saw on your knee – I've done this enough times to know it's both painful and a little humiliating.

Every tool kit needs a measuring tape or none of your cuts will ever match – cheap as chips is fine. It's a good idea to have several different-sized screwdrivers, both Philips and flat-headed types. I always pick mine up at car boot sales for pennies. A good hammer with a solid handle is essential around the house and garden. I like wooden handles as they are easier on the wrist.

Several G-clamps means needing one less pair of hands when cutting, but they're probably even more important for gluing things together. A multi-tool, such as a Leatherman, is a good all rounder, invaluable for dismantling things in skips. A gimlet set is another good buy – with a gimlet you can have a screw hole started in less time then it takes to get the electric drill out. The other great tool is a wrecking bar – good for getting pallets apart and for levering up floor boards.

Screws and nails

Nails can be used for permanent fixings, but screws tend to be more useful. If you ever want to disassemble your work, you must use screws.

Above: How I make my world. Rip saw, several hammers, folding ruler, drill, nails, G-clamp, various screwdrivers and the short, wooden-handled thing's a bradawl, or awl, for making holes.

Sourcing the best: costing the least

Free materials

The street is a truly amazing resource for material. Salvaging is a fantastic way of finding useful and interesting bits and pieces. I've found tools, soil, plants, arbours, watering cans, wheelbarrows, and seed tins – not to mention floorboards, skirting boards, gravel boards and all sorts of wood to make things for my garden. It's about seeing beyond the current state of the object and imagining something new. People throw out the most amazing stuff and it's a shame to let anything useful go to the landfill mountain.

Skip diving

By using stuff from the streets you not only lessen your own global footprint, but also that of those around you. It's a very thrifty way to get a lovely garden. But there are a few essential rules for getting stuff for free. Skip diving sits in a murky world of legal issues. It's a fact that people are throwing stuff out and therefore they don't want it, but they still have legal rights to it.

Always ask permission before you raid a skip, for two reasons: it's polite and it keeps you on the right side of the law. Many people are a little afraid of skip divers. In their eyes you're doing something very subversive. Mostly they are worried that you are dumping stuff in someone else's skip rather than taking it out. If you politely explain what you want and why, it will put people's minds at rest. And once people know what you're up to they may even save you stuff.

If you can't find anyone to ask permission from, leave a note. I've found it works wonders just to leave a note asking 'Is this wood being thrown out and can I have it? Tick Yes or No'. Some people swear by

diving only at night or early morning, mainly because they are less likely to run into anyone, but I reckon this looks suspicious. I dive at any time of day, I always leave the skip tidier than when I left it and I've yet to get into trouble.

Buying online

If you can't find your material from the street, eBay can be a fantastic source. You'll often find amazing stuff if you search very locally (10-mile radius) as the lists will be full of finds that people can't send in the post. The internet also lists sites with the best deals for bulk buying of screws, nails and other tools needed to transform your scrap. They'll be on your doorstep before you know it. Screwfix (www.screwfix.co.uk) is a good starting point for cheap fixings and tools.

Freecycle and Craig's list

Freecycle has been so useful that I wonder how we survived without it. You join your local online group and post things you want to get rid of. It's a first-come, first-served basis, offering such weird and wonderful things as train tickets, ceiling roses and paper. It is of course hit and miss, but you can find sheds, greenhouses, soil, turf and all sorts of plants that people have propagated. So if you find yourself with too many tomato seedlings or more beans then you know what to do with – offer them away.

Craig's list is a non-commercial (so no silly banners) network for online communities. Like Freecycle, you search by your area; it's better for cities than rural areas. It features barter, sales and wanted ads, as well as gigs, services and other community things, and has some good, topical discussion forums.

Skip-diving etiquette

Ask before you dive.

If you are confronted, walk away.

Never trespass – there will be another skip somewhere else.

Skips on people's drives are definitely out of bounds, unless you can see if they are in and ask them.

Always wear gloves, sturdy shoes and long trousers for diving (unlike me, but it was a very hot day). Skips are full of broken glass and rusty nails.

Keep a screwdriver or multi-tool in your backpack or handbag. Brass hinges, bolts and screws are really worth taking.

Keep looking. It's rare to find what you want immediately – it's an endlessly addictive trawl.

Keep karma on your side. Do not take for the sake of it, there might be someone else desperate for that find that's just going to sit in your garage.

Leave the skip tidy – if you take anything out that you don't want, put it back.

Let people know you're on the look out for wood, planters, window frames and suchlike. Word of mouth and tip-offs lead to the best finds.

Free seeds

If you really get into sowing, seed-swapping events are the best way forward. They're where you can get hold of lots of free seeds. You just take your surplus seeds along and swap them for other ones you want. If you don't have anything to swap yet, most seed exchangers are very accommodating to new gardeners. Look out on noticeboards in your area for spring events, or your local organisation may advertise online. If you Google 'seed swapping', you'll not only discover local events, but also a whole online community of year-round seed swappers. Seedy Sundays (www.seedysunday.org) is a UK-based site that has a list of events and also advises you how to set up your own group. Also look on Yahoo Groups under seed exchange.

Boot sales

Car boot sales are an excellent source of materials. For interesting, cheap plants, start hunting at boot sales from the end of spring and at the beginning of summer. This is when happy-go-lucky propagators have found they've got far too many plants and will start selling them off. I've found some really unusual stuff, even rare orchids.

They are also great places to find good tools. The last remnants of house and shed clearances from old relatives often end up at boot sales, and old spades and forks are often better than new. They tend to be made out of proper tempered steel and were built to last. You often find old spades and forks with dodgy handles; this isn't a problem as a good ironmonger will fit you a new one. Keep an eye out for hoes – the more worn the hoe is the better it works.

Support your local, independent ironmongers

If you're lucky, you will still have a local, independent ironmonger nearby, one of the best resources there is. These are people who have built up their business to support people like you and have a wealth of DIY expertise. Unlike the giant sheds that only want to sell you packets of things, you can go and buy that single screw you need. My local ironmongers, York Supplies, are a fantastic source of inspiration and never bat an eyelid when I ask for any advice, from the right size of drill bit or screw for a particular project to ways to preserve a piece of wood that's been sitting around in water for goodness knows how long.

Favourite online resources

Seed companies

Franchi Seeds www.seedsofitaly.com
Italian, beautifully packaged, generous quantities of
seed at good prices and heirloom varieties. The first
seed company to join the Slow Movement and you
can skype them for free – what's not to love?

Nicky's Seeds www.nickys-nursery.co.uk
Unusual and exotic seeds shipped around the world.
Good site packed with information. Nice, low-key
packing for seeds.

The Real Seed Catalogue www.realseeds.co.uk
No hybrids, no GMOs, just real, open-pollinated seed
so you can save your own. Really good resource on
how to harvest your own seed and nice generous
packages.

Thompson and Morgan
www.thompson-morgan.co.uk
Worldwide seed company, a bit old school, but with a
growing organic side. Difficult site to navigate, but tips
and guides section is full of useful stuff about
germination, planting times and harvesting.

Chilterns Seeds www.edirectory.co.uk/chilternseeds/
Heirloom, rare and unusual seeds. Very old school, best
bedside-reading catalogue and bargain prices for last
year's stock. Seed can be pricey though, with only
small quantities in packets.

Garden Resources

Garden Organic www.gardenorganic.org.uk
First port of call for organic gardeners. Very good
seasonal and organic advice section. Worth becoming a
member of the charity for its superb magazine and
seed list.

Royal Horticultural Society www.rhs.org.uk
Great god of gardening in Great Britain. Useless
internal search engine, so best to search by googling
'RHS tree', 'RHS lettuce' and so on. This is an
amazing site once you get used to navigating it.

BBC Gardening www.bbc.co.uk/gardening
Lovely, friendly site, good on advice. Good allotment
forum and 'how to' videos, and home of my blog.

www.video.google.co.uk
Really cool resource. If you want a quick guide on
how to plant or prune – watch a video.

Instructables www.instructables.com
Billed as the world's largest show and tell. It's chock
full of off-beat projects – complete crafter heaven –
with a growing gardening section.

You Grow Girl www.yougrowgirl.com
Canadian-based site for the alternative gardener.
Particularly good forum for projects and a nice show
and tell section.

Guerrilla Gardening www.guerrillagardening.org
This site started off as a blog, but has turned into a
huge forum for those who care about neglected public
spaces. Great community section where you can find
out what's happening in your area and get involved.

the Directory

Deciding what to grow can be a bit daunting when you first start out. Even if you've narrowed it down to vegetables or flowers, how do you decide what to try first? Start with some of the following cheap and easy vegetables, herbs and flowers that are as happy in containers as they are in the ground.

Top vegetables

Beetroot

The lovely thing about beetroot is that they grow themselves, you can't fail to get a crop. Sow seeds roughly 2cm deep with 20cm between rows. In wet weather or wet soil, soak the seed overnight before sowing. You can sow them at the final picking distance – about 20cm – but I prefer to sow about 5cm apart and gradually thin, taking out young leaves for salads and small beets to eat as baby beetroots.

Beets bolt quickly in hot weather or when there isn't enough water. Sow bolt-resistant varieties.

Cultivars 'Chioggia' is an old cultivar with stripy white and red flesh. 'Boltardy' doesn't bolt easily, 'Forono' and 'Cylindra' are deep red, long types.

Swiss chard

Swiss chard is easy, pretty and adaptable. Handsome enough for the flower garden, you can eat it right up till the first frost, plus it grows in shade. Some cultivars have brightly coloured stems. Sow 1cm deep and 20cm apart, thinning to 45cm apart. If you are growing in a container, make sure it is at least 30cm deep. Harvest leaves from the outside, by pulling rather than cutting them, using thinnings for salads.

I've been lazy and left frosted plants in containers only to get a second flush of leaves in spring before it went to seed.

Cultivars 'Rainbow Chard', 'Bright Lights' includes red, orange, yellow, purple and pale green stemmed plants.

Potatoes

It's easy to think that potatoes aren't worth bothering about. They are readily available, cheap, often local and if you've ever seen a potato field, you might think you need a lot of space. Suprisingly, you can become a good potato grower with hardly any space and no bare soil. Potatoes are such prolific growers that they'll happily produce a good crop in an old compost bag, a bin or large pot. In a very small space, you can grow a decent crop of fresh new potatoes when the ones in the stores are at a premium. Potatoes are categorised according to how long they take to crop. Earlies take around 90 days, second earlies around 110 days and main crops up to 160 days. In limited space, grow earlies and second earlies – new potatoes.

Don't plant any old sprouted grocery-bag potato, but start your crop with seed potatoes from a garden centre, mail-order catalogues or a local Potato Day if you're lucky. These potatoes are actually cuttings (a bit of potato with an eye) that are certified against the main diseases that infect potatoes. These diseases can stick around for ages – think of the Irish Potato Famine – so be sure to start with good stock.

Most growers recommend chitting potatoes before you plant. Chitting is when you start the tubers (seed potatoes) indoors. The potato will start to sprout and, when the sprouts are around 2.5cm long and the weather is right, you plant them out. But I confess that I never bother.

The lazy way to grow spuds is to fill the bottom of a large (30 litre) container such as a dustbin with about 25–30cm of multi-purpose compost. Place at the most two potatoes on top and cover them with more compost. As they start to shoot up out of the compost, cover them with more compost. Keep doing this till you have reached the top of your container. If you are growing in plastic bags, roll down the bag at the beginning and roll it up as you go along – don't forget to punch some holes at the bottom for drainage. Potatoes need water, especially if they are in

Top ten tips for healthy vegetables

1. Choose a sunny spot. Few vegetables like the dark. Parsley, mint, mizuna, spinach and Swiss chard will cope in light shade.

2. In the ground, specific families of vegetables need to be grown in a different part of your garden each year – in rotation. The four basic groups are legumes (beans and peas), potatoes, onions, and brassicas. Never follow like with like.

3. Successional growing keeps you fully fed. If there are crops you particularly like, and you've got the space, sow them every two or three weeks from late spring until mid summer.

4. Water the seed row first, then sow. This way you won't water the weed seeds.

5. In wet, cold weather sow more shallowly to stop seeds rotting.

6. If water is an issue, concentrate on watering when the fruit begins to crop.

7. Brassicas (e.g. cabbages, kales and broccoli) do best in firm ground. Tread down the soil when you plant and keep firming soil around plants as they grow.

8. The larger the spaces between root vegetables, the bigger they grow.

9. Grow nectar-rich flowers among your vegetables to encourage beneficial insects. Pot marigolds, California poppies, echinaceas, poached-egg flowers and nasturtiums all attract friendly insects that eat pests.

10. Feed your soil with garden compost. Healthy soil means healthy plants.

containers. In hot weather you should water every day.

Growing potatoes in the soil is just as straightforward. Some books will try to blind you with arcane knowledge and put off all but the brave for life. But the greatest potato grower I know told me that in busy years he digs a hole about 20cm deep, fills it with all the weeds he's dug up from round about, puts his potato in, back fills it and that's it. If you've got ground to fill, space your potatoes roughly 30–40cm apart in rows 40–50cm apart.

Harvest potatoes once they finish flowering, when their leaves start to turn yellow and wilt. If you are growing in containers, tip the whole tub onto a groundsheet or a split plastic sack to stop the soil from going everywhere and sift through to find the potatoes. Use the old compost as mulch. Ground-grown potatoes are harvested by levering whole plants out with a fork and picking off the individual spuds. Store in a cool, dark space.

Cultivars My favourite new potato is 'Red Duke of York', with its lovely, deep purple flowers and delicious waxy taste. It is very early, so you can have it in and out and get another crop in its place.

'Swift' is a good early, floury potato for containers, good for roasting or baking.

'Anya', a cross between the knobbly 'Pink Fir Apple' and the all-rounder 'Charlotte' is a great salad potato and I've a childhood soft spot for the waxy, nutty French 'Ratte'.

Garlic

Many of the gardening fraternity will frown, but I admit I never buy special, horticulturally produced garlic. I just use whatever I've got in my pot in the kitchen. It's not tested against disease, but it is very cheap. I take the biggest, plumpest cloves and in late November I push them 8cm or so into the soil, in a pot or in the garden, flat end first. If your soil is very heavy, you can get away with much shallower planting, as long as they're covered by 2.5cm of soil. In snowy areas, try to plant them a bit earlier. Leave about 10cm between cloves and 20cm between rows. An open and light spot is best. If you want to buy horticultural garlic, remember to split the bulbs to plant single cloves.

I don't water garlic in the ground, but in pots you'll have to. By mid to late summer, when the leaves start to turn yellow, pull up the bulbs and you've got garlic. You must harvest before the leaves are wilted or the bulb will start to rot. Some years there is a lot of rust around (yellow pustules along the leaves and stems) so harvest your bulbs early if the stems are covered with rust, even if it seems too soon.

Garlic needs around ten days of cold to initiate bulb production, which is why it's best to get them in before Christmas, but you can plant as late as February. If you do that, you can harvest bulbs of delicious 'green' or 'wet' garlic in late summer. You use whole bulbs fresh – wonderful in soup.

If I'm not planting a delicious clove from some farmer's market, then I always go for 'Cristo'. It's the best all rounder – good taste, good size and stores well.

Tomatoes

Thanks to a greater interest in heirloom varieties, and online catalogues, there is no need to ever eat a watery, tasteless tom again. You don't have to stick to red, you could try yellow, pink, white, black, striped green, or orange and purple.

Tomatoes have three distinct growing habits. Indeterminate, or tall, types are best

for allotments, community gardens and those with space. Bush, or determinate, are best for pots and patios. Dwarf are for hanging baskets, windowsills and for edging borders. Tall ones need pinching out, staking and having their side shoots removed. Bush are sprawling plants that don't need any pinching or staking. If you're not going to be around a great deal for your toms, then go for bush, as they require less work.

Tomato seeds need heat to germinate, but they germinate fast and they are really tough – I've seen them come up in cracks in pavements. Even seeds from your tinned plum tomatoes will germinate just fine, but as most of these varieties come from warm climates you'll probably have to grow them under cover. Don't be tempted to germinate too many tomatoes though, five plants in a small garden or patio is plenty.

Wait until all signs of frost have passed before you put young plants out and you may still need to protect them through cool nights – placing cardboard boxes over small plants works well. If you want to grow them in rows in the ground, leave 45cm between plants and 60cm between rows. In pots, grow a single tomato to a large pot. Compost bags are a good cheap option; lie a bag on its side on the ground, so that it has maximum depth for root run, make some drainage holes along the base and plant two tomatoes per bag.

Tall varieties need staking as they can't support their own weight once they fruit. A good stake needs to be at least 120cm long, driven in well clear of the rootball. Tie around the stake tightly and loosely around the stem, just below a leaf. Once the first flowers appear and start setting fruit, start weekly watering with a liquid tomato feed – potash-rich comfrey or nettle tea is best for this.

You need to remove some side shoots on tall types to increase productivity. True leaves are at right angles to the stem and the ones that sit at 45-degree angles are the side shoots. If you rock the shoot back and forth, it will snap off without tearing the stem. Also remove any shoots that appear at the very base of the plant. You'll need to stop the plants when six or so trusses of fruit have formed, which is when you pinch out the top of the plant to stop it growing. When all the fruit are ripening well, you can remove half the leaves from the bottom to middle of the plant. This will help the tomatoes to ripen better.

In wet, warm summers, the chief tomato killer is blight. It starts with chocolate-brown patches on the leaves and leads to blackened stems and fruits. It kills quickly and a tomato that looked fine in the morning can be covered by night. Spraying with copper sulphate (Bordeaux mixture) can stave off the worst, but inevitably the crop is lost. It is very important not to home compost diseased plants.

If frost is on the horizon and you have any unpicked fruit, cover the whole plant with fleece or plastic film. Towards the end of the season you can pull a whole plant up by the roots and hang it indoors, the green ones will ripen on the plant.

Cultivars Best cherry toms: 'Gardener's Delight' (best starter tom); 'Sungold', 'Baxter's Early Bush'.

Standard: 'Alicante', 'San Marzano'; 'Super Marmande' for pizza and passata, Heirloom: 'Green Zebra', 'Yellow Plum', 'Red Pear', 'Brandywine', 'Sebastopol'.

Dwarf types: 'Tiny Tom', 'Tumbling Tom Yellow', 'Tumbling Tom Red'.

Courgettes

Courgettes are great plants to start with. It's a myth that you need a lot of space because you don't need a lot of plants. Although they do need to be spaced 50cm apart in both directions in the ground, they will grow just as well in a large container, in compost bags or rubble bags, one plant to a bag. One plant will give you more courgettes then you know what to do with. Two courgettes will feed a family, three and you'd better find a courgette cake recipe!

There are round and long ones, and some that only produce flowers for stuffing. I'm fond of Italian cultivars and I like yellow ones because they look and taste good.

Always start courgettes in pots rather than straight into the ground as the risk of rotting seed is too great. Indoor germination definitely gives you a head start, sowing seeds a month before the last frost, but starting the pots outdoors means sturdy seedlings as seed germinates as the soil temperature rises. Plant out when you have two true leaves and a third on its way.

Courgettes often get mildew towards the end of a warm, damp season. Don't worry, healthy plants continue to produce plenty of fruit. Pick fruit when they are firm and small, large fruit turn to marrows and aren't good to eat. Twist at the base if you don't have a knife. The more you pick, the more the plant produces.

Cultivars My favourite is warty yellow 'Rugosa Friulana' – it's so ugly it's beautiful, and tastes divine.

'Jemmer' is prolific, reliable for beginners.

'Patty Pan' is a lovely scalloped squash, good raw in salads or stir fries.

Cucumbers

Cucumbers are classified as outdoor or ridge types – traditionally grown on ridges – and indoor types. Ridge types are tougher, with a greater resistance to pests, diseases and low temperature, so stick with them. Heirloom cultivars may have round or oval fruit – they're juicy and well-flavoured – and some have rough, prickly skins that need to be peeled before eating. Japanese or Burpless hybrids are smooth skinned, large and bred to be vigorous. Gherkins are sprawling smaller plants with fruit that can be eaten raw, but are mainly grown for pickling.

Cucumbers need at least 20°C to germinate and hate to be moved. Sow two or three seeds per pot and remove the weakest one after germination. Don't put them outside until there is a minimum temperature of 15°C. Cucumbers need plenty of light and moisture, but don't drown the seedlings. Harden off for at least two weeks in a cold frame, and plant out well after the last frost when there are two true strong leaves and a third of the way.

Grow cucumbers up a frame or tripod, tying in when necessary, and expect the plants to get 1.5-1.8m tall. Nip out the growth point when each plant reaches the top of its support. Cucumbers need to be well watered once fruit forms. Lay any lower fruits on a slate or piece of wood as soon as they appear so they don't sit on soil and rot. They won't withstand severe cold, so pick all fruit before frosts threaten.

Slugs love young plants, and aphids both eat them and transmit mosaic virus, which looks just as it sounds. Healthy plants can grow through mosaic virus, but yields are affected. Remove distorted leaves on older plants.

Cultivars 'Marketmore' (prolific and mildew resistant), 'Burpless Hybrid', 'Burpless Tasty Green'.

Heirloom: 'Crystal Lemon' and 'Crystal Apple'.

Peas, mangetout and petit pois

Peas are really pretty plants, perfect for patios. A single row or pot makes for good pickings for salads though you have to grow a lot for main meals. I love to make a salad of raw peas, spinach and really good feta cheese.

Peas are either suitable for winter sowing or for summer. Winter peas can be sown in October and early November to be ready for early June. If you are planting in pots, always choose dwarf or shorter varieties – some sugar snap peas grow up to 150cm and by the time you've staked the pot, the whole thing falls over. Sow summer crops every two weeks from April to June for a continuous supply. Sow peas 5cm apart, with rows twice that far apart. In a pot, I tend to plant in two concentric rings, with the stakes in between.

Mice love peas and will happily find and dig them up. To discourage them, you can either dip the peas in paraffin or buy a child's plastic snake and lay it on top of the soil. You'll need to move the snake every now and then, but since the mice come out at night they won't risk exploring to see if it's real.

Once pea seedlings appear, slugs will get them if you haven't laid appropriate defences. And they will need supporting from around 8cm tall. You can buy pea netting very cheaply and support it on posts, or make a wigwam of canes in a pot and wrap string around it. It's important to keep weeds down so mulch around young plants with a 5cm layer of grass mowings or cardboard, or keep on top of the weeding.

Water well in dry weather and pick peas from the bottom of the plant up. You can also eat the pea shoots at the very top of the growth raw in salads. When all the peas are picked, cut the plant, rather than pulling it up. The nitrogen-rich nodules on the roots will put goodness into the soil for the next crop.

Cultivars 'Oregon Sugar Pod' (very sweet) 'Meteor' (good for early sowings). 'Half Pint', 'Hatif d'Annonay' (dwarf).

Radishes

Radishes are the quickest crop, 6-8 weeks from sowing to eating, and you can start in February and continue to early September. They can seem to become a bit woody in summer so sow a new crop every ten days to a fortnight. Round radishes such as 'Cherry Belle' stay crisp longest. The first cropping tends to be very mild – hot radishes come later in the year.

You can slip in a short row of radishes whenever you get a bit of space in the ground, for example as you clear part of a row of lettuces, follow it up with a sowing of radishes. This is known as a catch crop. Sow seeds thinly in the ground, leaving about 15cm between rows, but scatter them liberally in containers and thin if you need to.

Radishes in the ground only need watering in the hottest weather. In pots, water them only when dry and, if they bolt, let plants go to seed and eat the pods.

Cultivars 'French Breakfast' (traditional red top and white bottom), 'Pink Beauty', 'Cherry Belle', 'München Beer' (edible seed pods).

French, haricot or kidney beans

Dwarf French beans are best for small gardens and pot culture as they need little or no staking and crop heavily. You can't sow French beans unprotected outside until well after your last frost as they hail from South America and need warmth to germinate. Cold, wet soil will rot seeds overnight. Indoors, you can start in pots in April and harden seedlings off before planting. Don't sow in trays or modules, but in pots at least 3cm deep because the beans are quick to put down big roots. Otherwise, sow 5cm deep in drills with around 25cm between beans, and at least 45cm between rows. A large 30-litre pot or wine box will take eight or so dwarf bean plants. If you sow two or three crops of French beans, three weeks apart until late June, you'll have beans to crop until September.

Cultivars 'The Prince' (high yields), 'Tendergreen' (high yields), 'Barlotto Lingua di Fuoco' (you can get both dwarf and climbing, so check the packet) is a lovely pink-podded, dwarf cultivar.

Carrots

Carrots need sandy soil and hate recently manured soils – stay off farmyard muck in your bed or container mix. Short, stumpy kinds like 'Paris Market' are great if you don't have big, deep pots. Long, lean types such as 'Amsterdam Forcing' or 'Nantes' will need deep root runs. Show carrots are traditionally grown in terracotta land drainpipes with lots of sand to get monster-length carrots. If you find a source of clay drains or chimney pots, grab them and grow normal-sized carrots instead.

Wait until April to sow carrots, and if you have space, remember to sow every few weeks until July for a regular supply. They take longer than one might expect to get to mature size. A May sowing won't crop until the end of August, although you can take baby carrots sooner.

Carrot seeds are tiny and difficult to sow evenly; try mixing seeds with sand in the palm of your hand before sowing to help spread the seed. The final distance between plants should be about 7cm and it's best not to sow too close as you don't want to thin too often. The chief pest is carrot fly, whose maggots can decimate a row of roots in no time. Carrot flies hunt out your carrots by smell and when you thin you invite them along as you waft carroty smells around. When you come to thin, do it on a cloudy day or in the evening and water the seedlings afterwards. Companion planting and barriers are good defences (see pp. 147–151).

Cultivars 'Paris Market Baron' or 'Paris Market' is a good stubby cultivar for containers. 'Early Nantes' is good for flavour and size, best in the ground.

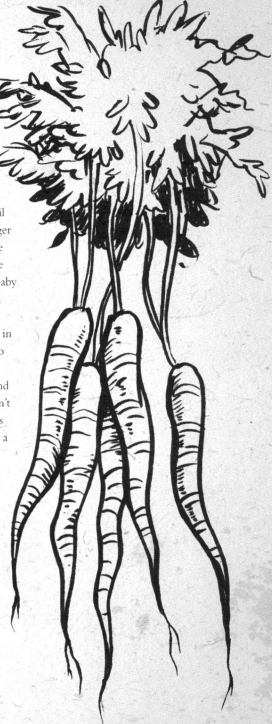

Your herb garden

Most garden centres sell small pots of perennial herbs very cheaply. These bulk up very quickly, so you'll be using them way before seed-sown plants. Look for thyme, tarragon, sage and rosemary, but sow seeds of basil and chives as you'll pay through the nose if you buy these as plants.

Parsley

Useful, tough, and pretty, parsley fares equally well in the ground and in pots. Everyone can have a pot to bring into the kitchen for winter. Curly-leaved moss parsley creates a mound of dark green leaves. French or Italian flat parsley is larger with superior flavour. It is best to treat parsley as an annual or biennial.

Parsley can be a brute to germinate, but it's worth the wait. It can take a month or two to show and throughout this period the soil must be kept moist. Speed the process up by pouring a kettleful of boiling water over the seeds once you've sown them, this should jump start germination. Parsley likes rich soil and can be sown as early as April and as late as August to have some plants to bring in for winter. Over-wintering parsley plants must be at least 20cm apart. Summer plants can be squeezed together, with about 8cm between them.

Basil

One of the most useful annual herbs. The laziest method is to use supermarket basil, separating each stem, pinching tops out and replanting. But there are all sorts of varieties to try, apart from the usual large-leaved green basil.

Basil needs warmth to germinate, 13–16°C, so sow indoors from March on a sunny windowsill or outside no earlier than May. On a windowsill sow into a 9cm pot, cover the seeds with a little compost and seal the pot in a clear plastic bag to keep moisture in. Remove the bag only once you see small seedlings. Transplant when large enough to handle. You'll need to harden off indoor plants in a cold frame before planting out. If outside sowings seem to be slow to germinate, water the ground a little as sometimes it's too dry to kick start germination.

'Sweet Genovese' has by far the best flavour for pesto and salads. Greek or bush basil has tiny, pungent leaves and forms an attractive light green mound. It seems to withstand cold and the wet summers other basils hate; even slugs and snails don't trouble it as much and it is very late to flower, so you get a large crop of leaves first. Thai basil is liquorice flavoured with purple and pink flowers and purple-tinged leaves, pretty enough to hold its own in window boxes or flower gardens. Lemon basil is tricky in anything but the best conditions, but delightful on a sunny kitchen window.

Sage

Sage is an evergreen perennial, great for the kitchen and lovely with your flowers. Purple-leaved sage makes a particularly attractive backdrop in your beds. Pineapple sage and tangerine sage are pretty in beds and even better made into fruity herb teas.

Cuttings or small plants (even the supermarket kind will tough it outdoors) are the easiest way to get sage established. Take 8cm long, stem-tip cuttings in April or May from friends' plants and root these around the edge of a 12cm pot in free-draining potting compost. Keep plants in the cold frame until rooted.

Although sage is perennial, it tends to get leggy and wear itself out, or if it favours a particular spot it can get huge. So either take cuttings or prune ruthlessly in spring.

Marjoram (oregano)

Cultivated forms include sweet marjoram, which only survives a winter in a warm climate, and the reliable perennial pot marjoram. It needs a fairly rich soil and full sun, and can be sown indoors from March and outdoors from May. It can be slow to germinate so be patient, you won't get a crop until the end of the summer. The hungry or impatient should bypass the seed stage by buying cheap plants. Once you have an established plant it's easy to make more by dividing your clump in spring or autumn, or taking cuttings in early summer.

Marjoram dies back in winter, but if you're growing it in a container cut the whole plant back hard in summer and bring the pot indoors for winter. That way you'll get a fresh flush of leaves for winter cooking.

Chives

Chives are easy to grow from seed sown indoors or out in late spring and early summer, you'll be picking by midsummer. You can also cheat, starting with cheap supermarket chives in pots. Plant these out in early summer and with luck they will adapt to life outside. Chives die back in winter, but are hardy enough to make it through all but the worst winters.

Mint

Spearmint, peppermint, apple, grapefruit, pineapple, Moroccan, woolly-leaved and variegated – there are so many mints. All are perennial, most are extremely tough and many rampantly invasive. The best thing about mint is that it will take shade, so if all you have is a north-facing windowsill, get into mints. Mint is happy in pots, but prefers moist, fertile soil so keep it well watered.

If you can't get a root or two from a friend, sow mint from April to May on a windowsill at about 15–20°C. Cover seeds with a fine, sieved layer of compost and transplant when your seedlings are large enough to handle. Once things have warmed up, plant outside in June. To avoid mint taking over your garden, restrict its roots by sinking an old pot or bucket into the ground and plant into this.

Thyme

Thyme is another perennial that's great for a neglectful gardener. It doesn't mind drought, poor soils and baking sun. Even in a pot, it will survive abuse that has most other herbs giving up the ghost. Lemon thyme is beautifully scented, but hates cold, wet winters. Broad-leaved thyme is the toughest and the most common. If you buy plants, check you're getting an edible kind as they are many, many varieties out there and some really don't taste good. Thyme is cheap and easily available from the garden centre, but it's quickest from cuttings or divisions in spring or autumn if you have a friend with a tasty variety. Plant outside from April onwards.

The trick with thyme is to cut plants back hard in June, this way you get a second flush of young, bushy growth for the rest of summer. If you have inherited a leggy thyme, cut it back hard in spring – apart from one leggy stem which you should bury in good compost (just chuck it over the plant so that a few leaves poke out). You'll be surprised how quickly it will rejuvenate.

Rosemary

Rosemary has delicate blue to palest blue flowers much loved by bees so it's a lovely addition to any garden. It is a hardy, perennial shrub that will grow to a great size if left to its own devices, or you can choose a prostrate form to cover the ground. Pink- and white-flowered rosemaries exist, but I don't think anything beats the traditional pale blue.

Rosemary likes very well-drained soil and full sun. It is just as happy in a pot as in the ground. Most streets have at least one rosemary in a front garden, so go make friends with your neighbours and ask for cuttings. If you have an overgrown plant that is still vigorous rather than woody, cut all stems back by at least half in mid spring and you'll get attractive, bushy growth, but if you inherited a really woody plant, you're better off taking cuttings and starting again.

Tarragon

French tarragon is a fine herb that takes your cooking up a step or two. Tarragon thrives in full sun, in well-drained soil – think south of France. In cold winters or on poorly drained soil, tarragon sheds its leaves, sulks and then gives up the ghost. Offer it some protection from the rain and cold – a really large water bottle used as a cloche works well – or find a very sheltered, dry spot as cold, wet conditions do the most harm.

It is not easy from seed, so either buy a plant or get hold of an underground runner or late spring cuttings from a friend. Don't be fobbed off with Russian tarragon, it's not the same flavour at all.

Favourite easy flowers

Godetia *Clarkia amoena*

I think godetias are considered a bit naff by the horticultural fraternity, but I love them, especially the pure pink ones. The reason I really like them is because in the wettest summer they'll flower their socks off, and yet they'll do the same in a baking hot year. Direct sow these annuals by scattering them over a prepared seedbed, then gently raking them in. They'll do the rest. They look a bit like an evening primrose flower, but come in a variety of acid tones – brash, but beautiful.

Morning glory *Ipomoea purpurea*

Morning glory is a beautiful annual vine, closely related to the beastly bindweed – but it doesn't take over because it dies back each winter. It loves hot summers, so give it a trellis in a baking corner and once it starts flowering it won't stop till the first frosts. I'm fond of the traditional purple trumpets with pink centres, but there are dozens of colours to choose from.

You can direct sow, but morning glory likes a week or more's continuous warm weather to germinate so it's usually better to start it off on a warm windowsill or in an airing cupboard. There germination will be quick and, the minute you see green shoots, move the pots or trays somewhere a little cooler. Plant out from late May and give the plants a structure to clamber up.

Cornflower *Centaurea cyanus*

A tall, upright annual much loved for its clear blue flowers. It is perfect for filling sunny gaps in new gardens where it will often freely seed to come up year after year. It generally flowers in early summer, but sometimes it does the opposite and flowers in late August.

The wild blue cornflower is an attractive plant in its own right. Cultivars such as 'Frosty Mixed' have rather larger blooms in colours ranging from pale pink to deep purple. All do best on fairly poor soil; if it's too rich they flop. Sow direct into the soil, 1cm deep, either in autumn or as soon as the soil has warmed up in spring. You don't need to thin or feed them and they make lovely cut flowers.

Mountain cornflower *Centaurea montana*

One of the easiest flowers to please, centaurea has a generous spreading habit and is covered with blue and purplish cornflower-like blooms from late spring right through summer – with a bit of deadheading. It will tolerate very poor soils and a fair amount of shade. It's a self seeder, so once in your garden it tends to move itself around. It has deep, rhizomatous roots, so it can be a bit of pain to get rid of if you decide you don't like it.

Love-in-the-mist *Nigella* species and *Nigella papillosa* 'African Bride'

Another generous flower that will spread itself around once it gets established. Love-in-the-mist is a hardy winter annual so you can scatter seed in autumn, forget all about the snow and frost and still find seedlings in spring. It has star-shaped flowers, from sky blue to deep purple, and a cloud of fluffy, pale green foliage, but most people know it best for its attractive, inflated seedpods. It makes a lovely cut flower at every stage, but I like to leave the seedheads for winter interest. There are white, pink, purple and blue forms, but you won't go wrong with the wild form. I'm fond of the cultivar 'African Bride', which is white with deep maroon stamens.

Nasturtium *Tropaeolum majus*

Nasturtiums will do their best to climb so you can train plants over a fence, but I think they look best scrambling and make an ideal summer ground cover. Nasturtiums are cheerful, drought-hardy, and they thrive in poor soils, plus you can eat the flowers – and the foliage. Don't feed them or you'll get more leaves than flowers.

Nasturtiums can tough it out almost anywhere so they're ideal for window boxes and hanging baskets. Sow the seed direct from April to June, just under 2.5cm deep, and keep the soil moist until the seedlings appear. Once the seedlings are large enough to handle, you can thin to 30cm apart and you'll get really big bushy plants and flowers from June to October. Nasturtiums come in lots of different colours from palest yellow to deep, dark red and some really garish ones with variegated foliage. Some forms scramble, some are dwarf and bushy.

Sweet peas *Lathyrus odoratus*

The trick with annual sweet peas is to sow a batch in autumn and another batch in spring, this way you will have a great display and picking from mid summer through until the frost.

Sweet pea seeds look just like peas. Your gran will no doubt tell you to soak them, but in fact this is pointless. For autumn sowing use pots at least 8cm deep, sow two seeds per pot about 1cm down – toilet roll tubes make handy pots for the deep roots, but you may not want these hanging about for months. Ideally seedlings can be overwintered in a cold frame to plant out at the end of April.

You'll need to guard against slugs, mice and pigeons in particular. In spring, sow outside in the flowering position any time from March on, as long as the soil is not too cold. Or sow early March inside as for autumn sowings in pots.

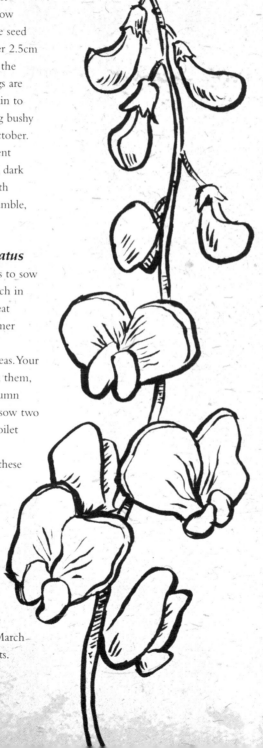

When seedlings are 10cm or so, pinch out the growing tips to get bushier plants.

Give sweet peas a good support such as a wigwam with string wrapped around it. You may need to tie them in from time to time. The more you pick, the more they'll flower. Sweet peas don't like to be too dry or they'll get mildew and stop flowering. The richer the soil, the better the plant. If growing in the ground, dig in some home-made compost a couple of weeks before planting out – this will conserve moisture and give an added boost.

Many of the modern hybrids are scentless, so make sure you pick a packet that says it's scented. 'Matucana' and 'Cupani' have particularly strong scent and lovely bicoloured maroon flowers.

Sunflowers *Helianthus* spp.

These days, sun-loving sunflowers come in many more hues than the traditional yellow. 'Velvet Queen' is a rich dark orange annual and, at the other end of the spectrum, is the perennial 'Lemon Queen', which has palest lemon-yellow flowers.

Most sunflowers are cultivars of the fast-growing *Helianthus annuus*. There are short sunflowers for windowsills and extra-tall ones for children. I like to sow mine in pots because slugs are very partial to young seedlings. Sow between April and early June (staggered sowing gives staggered flowering), 2–3 cm deep, in good potting compost. Plant as close as 15cm apart if you want to screen off an ugly wall or 30cm apart for bushier plants, and keep them well watered. Sunflowers make very good, long-lasting cut flowers.

When they've flowered, you can either be generous and leave the seedheads for the birds, who'll quickly devour them come late autumn, or you can chop off the heads and eat the seeds yourself. Whatever your preference, save some for sowing next year.

English or pot marigolds
Calendula officinalis

Bright orange marigolds bloom almost continually from early summer right the way through to late autumn. They are edible and pretty in salads and can also be cut for the vase. In mild climates, marigolds act as short-lived perennials and you can cut back old stems to get new growth. In colder climates, treat them as annuals – marigolds produce dozens of curved seeds per plant and self seed freely, or it's easy to collect the seed and scatter it around. If you're using them to edge a border or grow in tubs, sow seeds 2cm deep after frost in the final flowering positions.

Annual poppies – *Eschscholzia* and *Papaver* spp.

The California poppy (*Eschscholzia californica*) has lovely, clear orange flowers and attractive, fern-like, greyish foliage. It loves sun and doesn't mind drought – perfect for gravel gardens or baked, sunny areas. Direct sow in warm spring soils. Rake the area and sow seed, thinly 6mm deep. It needs 15-18°C to germinate.

I never bother to thin, just let the strongest muscle it out. Breeders have been developing California poppies for around a century, so there are dozens of colours out

there. Just choose what will go with your colour scheme. I particularly like the palest yellow 'Alba' and the deep pinkish carmine 'Carmine King'. Once established, most clumps will re-seed themselves each year.

The Shirley poppy is a selected form of the wild field poppy (*Papaver rhoeas*). The true Shirley Series have single flowers in clear shades of white, rose and salmon, but there are all sorts of strains on the market. Some are lovely, some not. 'Mother of Pearl' has particularly pale flowers. Sow direct, which simply means throw handfuls around in recently raked soil.

The opium poppy (*Papaver somniferum*) is a large annual, 1–1.5m tall, with fleshy grey leaves, large flowers and prominent seedheads. The large selection includes double or paeony-flowered forms, and colours from dark purples and pinks right through to white. Most have a deep purple to black staining in the centre. The darkest is 'Black Paeony' with deep purplish black, double flowers, the palest 'White Cloud' with pure white flowers. The trick with bountiful amounts of seed – seed swapping events always have bags of it – is to throw a handful out each week from February to May.

First published in Great Britain in 2008 by
Kyle Cathie Ltd
122 Arlington Road, London NW1 7HP
general.enquiries@kyle-cathie.com
www.kylecathie.com

10 9 8 7 6 5 4 3 2 1

978 1 85626 777 9

Editorial Director: Muna Reyal
Designer: Carl Hodson
Copy editor: Charlie Ryrie
Photographer: Simon Wheeler
Illustrator: Aaron Blecha
Production Director: Sha Huxtable

A Cataloguing In Publication record for
this title is available from the British Library.

Colour reproduction by Sang Choy
Printed and bound in China by SNP Leefung

For Emily Casstles

Acknowledgements
To those behind the book: Muna, Carl, Aaron and the lovely,
patient Charlie – thank you. The book is made brilliant in my
mind by the lovely Mr Wheeler's pictures – thank you for
both those and the long lunches.

I am lucky to have a lot of people around me that make
things, create stuff, write, doodle, knit, paint and garden in
such a way that it is an endless source of inspiration to me.
It is this community as much as me that made this book.
So here goes:
Clare Savage for reading early drafts, creating funny knitting
and taking me to gigs when it all got too much; my mother
for her lovely home-made frozen dinners; Dad, Becca and Jon;
Rose and the Gardeners' World team; the worm lady; Silvia;
Cary in NY; Jake Price; John and Elka, the original wine-box
growers; Juliet Glaves; Beth and Sid; Helen; Steph; Mags and
Ronnie; Emily C; Beryl and her team at North One Garden
Centre; John and his team at York Supplies; Anna Dennis;
Borra; Sue and Les for putting up with all the banging next
door and the Mighty D for pertinent advice, including 'how
to start a book'. To two I've never met, but oh do I love their
writing: Joy Larkcom and MFK Fisher. And lastly but not
least, there are three people that really put up with a lot while
I wrote this book: Joseph and Geoff whose make, do and bang
together advice was invaluable. They're also pretty cool to
work with. Most of all to Holiday, I love you and
the beautiful things you make. Oh, and the dog.